Henderson's Heroes

NICKY HENDERSON

Henderson's Heroes

THE STORY OF AN UNBELIEVABLE SEASON

Foreword by

James Nesbitt

RACING POST

First published in Great Britain in 2013 by
Racing Post Books
Axis House, Compton,
Newbury, Berkshire, RG20 6NL

10 9 8 7 6 5 4 3 2 1

A catalogue record for this book is available from the British
Library.

ISBN 978-1-909471-18-4

Cover designed by Jay Vincent
Designed by J. Schwartz & Co.
www.jschwartz.co.uk

Printed and bound in the UK by Butler Tanner & Dennis, England

www.racingpost.com/bookshop

Photographic acknowledgements

Nicky Henderson: pages 13, 83 and 179;
cranhamphoto.com: pages 6, 14, 18, 26, 28 (top), 48, 49, 51 101 and 103;
Fiona Crick: pages 17, 24–25, 44–45, 84, 88, 116–17 and 120;
Getty Images: pages 66, 127 and 143;
John Grossick: page 119.

CONTENTS

1

2

3

4

5

6

James Nesbitt with Riverside Theatre after the Ascot Chase in February 2012.

FOREWORD

by James Nesbitt

PENWOOD FORGE MILL and Boomerang were two of my
first loves. As a child I'd sit with my mother, glued to the
small screen, watching in wonder as, under the stewardship of
Paddy McMahon and Eddie Macken, these magnificent horses
performed their heroics at the Horse Of The Year Show. That
is how my love of horses, and of jumpers in particular, began.

Over the years I'd keep a keen eye on steeplechasing,
but it was when I first visited the Cheltenham Festival in
1988 that I was gone. Solid gone. It had everything: the
beauty and character of the horses; the courage of the
jockeys; the gathering of tens of thousands of people from
all backgrounds, bearing witness to this most extraordinary
spectacle; the triumph and the despair; the losing betting
slips and crumpled hearts – and, of course, the Irish.

Twenty-four years later, to be standing in the winner's
enclosure at Cheltenham having won the Ryanair Chase
with Riverside Theatre under a stupendous ride from Barry
Geraghty was ridiculous, magical, and essentially down to
one man: Nicky Henderson, whom I'd met a few years earlier
through Brian Stewart-Brown, himself a keen and successful
owner. Nicky is engaging and witty, mischievous and articulate.
He and I bonded immediately, and when the opportunity came
to acquire a horse to be trained at Seven Barrows, Brian, I and
two friends – pardon the pun – jumped.

Nicky's record speaks for itself, but to go down to his yard
and see him at work is to witness something other-worldly,
something miraculous. He treats his horses as you would your
children. Firm, at times, but never without respect, pride and
unconditional love. And he knows them, their characters and
all their individual idiosyncrasies better than anyone.

To get Riverside Theatre right for Cheltenham in 2012 was
one of the great training feats, and I'll be forever grateful.

Nicky is unique.

PREFACE

by Andrew Pennington, *Racing Post*

AT THE CLOSE of the 2012–13 jumps season Nicky Henderson became champion trainer for the first time in 26 years, with a stellar collection of stable stars – notably Sprinter Sacre, Bobs Worth, Long Run and Simonsig – producing a succession of big-race wins.

So exhilarating was Nicky's domination of the season that we at the *Racing Post* decided we must produce a permanent record of his feat by putting together a book derived from the unrivalled reporting and photographic resources of the newspaper. The idea was so wholeheartedly received by the trainer himself that this book, though far from a conventional autobiography, is a worthy expression of what has made Nicky Henderson one of the greatest trainers of all.

The book begins with a revealing interview in which Nicky tells the *Racing Post*'s senior feature writer Steve Dennis about his life and career, taking us through his early years with a trainer's licence; the stars such as See You Then and Remittance Man; the move from Windsor House to Seven Barrows; and his resurgence in form in recent years with such horses as Champion Hurdle winners Binocular and Punjabi.

But 2012–13 brought his reputation to fresh heights, and an account of that magical season as chronicled in the *Racing Post*, forms the core of the book, with Nicky providing a commentary full of fascinating insights into life at Seven Barrows.

Complementing the text is a stunning array of photographs by the *Racing Post*'s Edward Whitaker, plus images from Nicky's private collection and pictures taken by Fiona Crick, who spends countless hours at Seven Barrows.

Thanks to John Randall for his assistance in collating the statistics, and to Sean Magee for his invaluable advice throughout the project. And, finally, this book could not have been completed without the enthusiasm and support of Nicky himself in providing the story behind what was his *annus mirabilis*.

INTRODUCING NICKY HENDERSON

by Steve Dennis

Previous spread: Relaxing at Seven Barrows, my home since 1992.

HE LOOKS REFLECTIVELY into his glass, a glass that he would characteristically regard as half full. Nicky Henderson is in the mood to tell stories, has sailed entertainingly through his vast repertoire, has saved the best until last like the seasoned professional he is.

Before he begins the best story, the last story, he pulls himself up short as though something has crossed his mind, and that familiar smile crosses his face again. 'It's been bloody good fun all the way, which is how it's supposed to be,' he says, reducing the great years, the good years and the not-so-good years into a portable philosophy that all those connected with him will recognise, will have shared in. Bloody good fun all the way.

All the way from the beginning, and the first flowering of stories. He might have been lost to racing before he started, given that the usual route through life for an Old Etonian does not correspond to the road less travelled yet enthusiastically trodden by the man himself, who chuckles at the tale of his Great Escape.

'I got let out of the City,' he says, although there is more than a hint of his helping the jailer to turn the key. 'My father Johnny was a partner in Cazenove, the stockbrokers, and that was what I was supposed to do too.

'I did a year and a half there but I'd have been no good for them, although my brother Harry had a great career there instead. Dad had a financial brain, and I don't. On the other hand, Dad was a very important man for racing, a special man for racing, and I'd always ridden and I'm sure I'd have done something involved with horses whether I stayed in the City or not.'

His father Johnny was instrumental in the salvation of both Cheltenham and Aintree, the twin jewels of

Clockwise from right: With my parents, Johnny and Sarah, brother Harry (middle) and sister Josie at West Woodhay; leading up one of Dad's point-to-pointers at an Easter Monday meeting at Lockinge; and an early riding experience at home.

Fred Winter: legendary jump jockey and trainer.

steeplechasing, when the dark shadow of the developers loured over those courses in the 1960s and 1980s respectively. The City might have been the intention but the underlying inheritance was the world of racing, and following his mother's death in a tragic accident in the hunting field – 'We were all in a bit of a muddle at the time' – his life took a new direction.

The family home at West Woodhay is not so far from Lambourn, and in 1973 he moved there to work as assistant trainer to the legendary Fred Winter at a time when the yard was at its very highest ebb. The two cornerstones of the house that Nicky built are his father and Winter, and the foundations that Winter laid down for his blue-eyed, rosy-cheeked apprentice are still visible despite the passing of 40 years of accumulated wisdom.

'It was a magical time – we had Bula, Pendil, Lanzarote, Crisp, and later on Midnight Court,' he remembers, invoking a list of horses whose deeds still inform the appreciation of jump racing even at this remove. He absorbed a lifetime's knowledge at the knee of the master, absorbed an affection for Lambourn that has lasted a lifetime, and thus doubly armed took out a training licence of his own at Windsor House stables, in the centre of the little racing town, in 1978. He was very young to go it alone, just 27, and the initiative might have looked a youthful indiscretion given the circumstances.

Bula winning his second Champion Hurdle in 1972 under Paul Kelleway.

As close as I have come to winning the Grand National, and this was in my first year as a trainer! Zongalero (right), ridden by Bob Davies, at the last fence in 1979 with Rubstic (Maurice Barnes), who went on to win by a length and a half. Eight years later I had the runner-up again: The Tsarevich, who was beaten five lengths by Maori Venture.

'I'd ridden 75 winners as an amateur, won the Fox Hunters' around Aintree on Happy Warrior and the Imperial Cup on Acquaint, and I thought I might as well start training. I'd reached the stage where either I went to work for someone else or I went out on my own.

'But I'd learned the ropes with Fred and there wasn't anywhere better to go, and if I hadn't learned enough from him in five years I wouldn't have learned it anywhere else in 25. I rode Rolls Rambler to win the Horse and Hound Cup at Stratford that summer, hung up my boots and started training.'

A sunbeam smile is never far from the surface and he unleashes it now as he recalls his younger self, brave and bold and blessed with unshakable confidence. 'I started off with nothing, hardly anything anyway, started with zero, went from zero to Zongalero.

'I had Happy Warrior, who was over the top by then, as was Acquaint. Luckily there was also Zongalero, belonging to David Montagu, my very first owner. How in the world he decided on me, I've no idea, but I'm very grateful that he did because Zongalero was some horse to start off with.

We start early: Mick Fitzgerald and I had a long and successful association before he was forced to retire from the saddle in 2008. If he hadn't had that injury I have no doubt he would still be riding for me now. I know he misses it enormously, and I miss him. He was a wonderful stable jockey.

'There weren't many horses and there wasn't many of us – me, Diana, Corky Browne as head lad, Johnny Worrall as travelling head lad and Jimmy Nolan as conditional jockey. That was about it; yet we had 23 winners in our first season, which was quite amazing really.'

What is considerably more amazing than a double handful of winners whose names have been lost to history are the names that haven't. Henderson's remarkable success as a trainer has been characterised by the enduring relationships he has forged along the way, and it is this astonishing continuity that has enabled him to build again and again on past glories, build an empire. Corky Browne is still his head lad and a legend in his own lifetime; Johnny Worrall's tenure as travelling head lad came to an end only two years ago; ultra-capable Rowie Rhys-Jones is only his third secretary in 35 years and she has no intention of allowing there to be a fourth.

Jockeys have naturally come and gone, yet even here there has been a constancy of personnel that illustrates how Henderson is a man for the long haul, for steadiness rather than a quick fix. He names his senior jockeys on his fingertips – Bob Davies, Steve Smith Eccles, Richard Dunwoody,

*Is anybody listening?
Directing operations on the
schooling grounds.*

Mick Fitzgerald, Barry Geraghty – and needs just one
hand for all his right-hand men.

'I've enjoyed huge stability with the people I've had
working with me. They must all be very tolerant people!

'Obviously, the greatest additions to the team and the
household have been my three daughters Sarah, Tessa and
Camilla – although they're not now actively involved in racing
they've been a vital help and support to me both on and off the
racecourse. For the last four or five years Sophie has been an
absolutely integral part of the way everything runs smoothly, and
I couldn't do my job without everyone else doing theirs so well.

'I'm not the world's best delegator, it must be said, but I rely
heavily on the team around me. I don't muck out too many –
this isn't 1978 any more! But two or three times a week, at half
past five, with Corky and all my assistants, we go religiously
round and look at 140 horses, feel their legs, check their health.
It's very old-fashioned I suppose but that's how we do it. It takes
about an hour and a half and we learn new things all the time.'

During those early days at Windsor House he kept the
wheels turning without going anywhere fast. All young trainers
need a star name in the yard to help them stand out from the

See You Then and Steve Smith Eccles (near side) lead Gaye Brief and Richard Linley at the last flight before going on to a second Champion Hurdle success in 1986.

crowd, and Henderson's first great horse was triple Champion Hurdle winner See You Then; also his first great headache. See You Then was a learning curve all on his own – he had a temper that made him a devil at home and fragile tendons that made his public appearances few and far between – and Henderson learned the hard way.

'See You Then was our breakthrough horse, our first Cheltenham winner, bought by my marvellous vet Frank Mahon. But he was impossible in his box, so I owe a lot to his lad Glyn Foster, who looked after him from the day he arrived. I've still got the jerseys and jackets full of holes that tell the tale of going into his box. He either bit you or kicked you.

'I'll never forget one Sunday morning, after his Champion Hurdle prep at Haydock the day before. I'd been lying awake worrying about his legs, so I got up first thing and went to have a look at him. When I walked into the yard I could see the door of his box was open, and when I had a look inside I saw Frank sitting on the manger. He hadn't been able to sleep either and had come to check on the horse – but when he'd gone in See You Then wouldn't let him out, and he wouldn't let him take the bandages off either.

'Then he wouldn't let me out, and so there we both were, hoping like mad that it wasn't Glyn's Sunday off. It wasn't; eventually he came in and distracted See You Then long enough for us to escape. He was able to remove his bandages, and thankfully those legs were okay.'

See You Then – known as See You When by the headline-writers for his infrequent appearances – tested his young trainer's mettle. He was second in the 1984 Triumph Hurdle and returned to Cheltenham the following year to win his first Champion Hurdle, watched by his trainer from a manhole cover on the lawn in front of the grandstand – another long-serving aspect of the Henderson saga, it being the spot from which he has watched nearly every Cheltenham race since. Yet these victories were hard-won.

'He was such a difficult horse to train because of his legs. I couldn't run him that often, and the following year there was a freeze-up and we were harrowing the gallops at two-hour intervals through the night so that we'd be able to work him in the morning. I drove the tractor myself a lot of the time.

'Now and again we took him to the beach for exercise, and ten minutes before he left I'd have another horsebox leave the yard in the other direction to throw the press off the scent – they all wanted to see him work because he'd been off for so long, they didn't believe he was still alive! He was a wonderful, wonderful horse but he did give us some trouble.'

See You Then's period of dominance was accompanied by a blossoming of talent from Windsor House, the likes of Alone Success, River Ceiriog, First Bout, Rustle, Classified and The Tsarevich confirming their trainer as a man for a big race, the big occasion. Then along came the brilliant Remittance Man, winner of the Arkle Chase and the Queen Mother Champion Chase, to lend a flourish to the first half of Henderson's career.

He has reluctantly just come around to confirming the awe-inspiring Sprinter Sacre as the best he's trained – 'I have to admit that now. I was always trying to protect See You

Above: With our star chasers of the early 1990s Remittance Man (left) and Travado.

Left: Remittance Man and Jamie Osborne are led in by owner Tim Collins (wearing glasses), who was a great friend of my parents, and lad Ian Major after winning the Queen Mother Champion Chase in 1992. Our long-time travelling head lad Johnny Worrall (right) is showing off his famous Cheltenham Festival-winning salute, and David Minton is behind me.

Then, but Sprinter's in a different sphere' – but in Remittance Man he had a horse cut from similar cloth, and as quirky as See You Then if not nearly as irascible.

'He was an unbelievable, spectacular jumper, but a tiny little narrow thing, nothing to look at. We couldn't gallop him very much because he galloped himself, full of nervous energy. And he was a boxwalker – so we put a sheep in with him to keep him calmer. The sheep changed every year – the first year he had "Ridley Lamb", then it was "Allan Lamb", and the year after that it was Nobby.'

Nobby of undying fame. 'Unbeknown to us, Nobby and Remittance Man had developed the most extraordinary relationship. When Nobby had done his year and gone back to West Woodhay, back to the flock, we gave Remittance Man a different sheep. Five seconds later it came back over – over, mark you – the stable door, wool flying everywhere. He'd picked the sheep up in his teeth and flung it out.

'We shoved it back in, out it came again five seconds later, more wool everywhere. Remittance Man didn't want any old sheep; he wanted Nobby. I went to West Woodhay and said, "I need Nobby," and I was shown into a field containing

499 sheep and one Nobby – but which one? In the end we took a horse into the field and all the sheep ran away and one stayed: Nobby.'

Remittance Man's reign coincided with Henderson's move across Lambourn from Windsor House to Seven Barrows in 1992 – his first and certainly his last move. Having started out in Lambourn with Fred Winter, Henderson was not inclined to move elsewhere when Windsor House became too cramped for comfort, and did a secret deal with Peter Walwyn – 'No-one else knew what was happening, not the locals, not the press' – to switch stables. Seven Barrows has become almost a spiritual home for Henderson, a nirvana without the necessity of dying first, its wide-open spaces allowing him free rein to expand on all fronts.

'I wouldn't ever want to train anywhere else – I don't think I could, considering we're so spoilt where we are. We're practically in a little village of our own, it's a lovely place, I can go where I like any day of the week, never use a work-strip more than once a year, just move over a yard or two and always use fresh ground.

'Nearly all our work is done on grass rather than all-weather, grass that's never seen a plough in a thousand years. That's probably the reason that we have a lot of bumper winners – we can work the youngsters in big batches across a wide strip with an older horse in front showing them the way, then they form fours, then go up two by two. That approach teaches them racecraft and we wouldn't have the room to do it if we trained anywhere else.

'I feel as though I'm the curator of two things: Sprinter Sacre and Seven Barrows. The barrows are 4,000 years old – I'm just looking after the place for whoever comes next.'

The secrets of Henderson's success emerge piecemeal, parsed from the context of whichever story he's recounting. There is the continuity of the workforce, there is the blissful situation of a yard that allows him to pursue the craft of training with a dexterity denied his peers. There is, necessarily, an army of both budding and full-blown talent to win all those races, and in his elucidation of that aspect he unconsciously displays another of the factors that have underpinned his training life – patience.

Following the move to Seven Barrows his career plateaued – six or seven years went by without a headline horse, there were three blank years at the Cheltenham Festival, and even when a winner came there it was isolated in relatively minor company. Other trainers might have despaired, might have panicked, might have begun changing methods that had served them so well for so long. Not Henderson. He treated the trials of relative austerity with the same demeanour as he had the years of relative prosperity, and kept his hand steady on the wheel.

'The first few years here were probably my least successful years, but I wasn't particularly unhappy with things, just delighted about the move and what it would mean for us. I knew things would come right.

'Of course it was a case of getting used to the new place. I'd come off gallops that I'd been using for 20 years, that I'd got used to, and it took time to work things out here because different gallops make different demands on horses. And I probably didn't have a wonderful bunch of horses at the time, but it's all about finding one's feet.'

Perhaps it wasn't a wonderful bunch of horses, but here too innovation would solve that problem. The traditional focus has always been stock from Britain and Ireland, but Henderson – with the assistance of another band of long-term allies – began to cast his net across the Channel. It's an aspect of the job he relishes, he looks forward to shopping trips like a child counting down the days to a trip to Hamley's, and the process affords him the opportunity to include his owners in that 'bloody good fun' he mentioned earlier.

'The good horses have to be sourced, of course, and the big change came when we went French. Ireland was in boom-time and I couldn't afford the top horses, had no chance, even the average point-to-pointer was fetching silly money. I'd started out using Johnny Harrington of the Curragh Bloodstock Agency and still do, but David Minton was at the CBA at the same time and after he set up on his own we've worked together ever since.

'Minty's an integral part of the whole operation. We do all the buying together, work together at all the sales, and not a day goes by when we don't talk to each other about this horse or that – and he shares the delights and disappointments of that Cheltenham manhole cover with me!

Overleaf: The horses return to Seven Barrows on the all-weather gallop.

Anthony Bromley has been instrumental in sourcing horses for us from France and at the home sales, including Fondmort, Juveigneur, Punchestowns, Punjabi, Une Artiste, Zaynar and all of our Million In Mind Partnership horses.

'It was through him that our French connection was established. He and Anthony Bromley formed Highflyer Bloodstock and Anthony has been absolutely vital in developing a successful pipeline of horses from across the Channel. I can't stress enough how important that has been. The first batch of horses we bought from France included Geos [dual Tote Gold Trophy winner] and Katarino [1999 Triumph Hurdle].

'I have a great deal of fun buying horses, I love the sales – as long as I've got money to spend, and that's where my owners come in. I train for the very nicest people – it's got to be fun and with my owners it always is. That's where I'm very, very lucky. Maybe that's a little bit of the difference between the Flat and the jumps.

'I tell them that I'll look after the business side, all the worrying and the working, and you just come along and have a good time. So many of my owners have been with me for years – I trained a winner ridden by Robert Waley-Cohen, that's how long I've known him!

'We all get along and enjoy it, and Sophie is brilliant at looking after the owners. I'm a very bad procurer of owners – I'm of the view that if someone wants a horse with you, they'll come to you, and I'm lucky that people do. It's open house, really, for the owners, they can turn up every day of the week to see their horses. That's the kind of set-up I prefer to have and my owners are a huge asset to me.'

The better horses began to come along, like Stormyfairweather (the second one Henderson had for Christopher and Bridget Hanbury), Fondmort, Marlborough and Trabolgan – 'one of the many good horses for Trevor Hemmings, who has been a fantastic supporter for many years' – and they brought the bigger races with them, yet everyone involved in racing knows that where horses are involved the joy they bring is always darkly marbled with the heartbreak of injury and worse. The even flow of jaunty stories, jovial stories, uplifting stories dries up as the mood darkens, as Henderson's heart appears on his sleeve, as the story of The Proclamation becomes inevitable.

'We've lost a lot of good horses along the way, but the truth of it is that it doesn't matter how good they are. If that

Geos winning the first of his two Tote Gold Trophys at Newbury in 2000 with Mick on board.

part of the job is an occupational hazard, it's one you don't get over very easily. It creases you. Oh, I thought he was a magical horse.'

The Proclamation was a shooting star, a comet so bright that when Henderson closes his eyes he can surely see him still imprinted on his vision almost 25 years on. It was a short life and sweet and so bittersweet.

'Michael Buckley has been in my life a very long time, and I rang him on my way back from Ireland to say I'd seen the most spectacular horse and that its next owner is either you or Sheikh Mohammed, who was briefly involved in jumping at that stage.

'We left The Proclamation with Paddy Prendergast jnr, he won at Punchestown, then came over to me and won his first novice chase by 15 lengths. I phoned Buckles and said, "If you want to stay novice chasing, that's fine, but if you want to go over hurdles, he'll win you the Champion Hurdle." Well … we decided to stay novice chasing, and three weeks later he went to Ascot, did the splits, broke his back.

Three of my greatest moments with Mick:

Fondmort winning the Tripleprint Gold Cup in December 2002: Mick said he had never jumped a final fence so high. Fondmort adored Cheltenham and won four chases there, including the Ryanair Chase in 2006.

Trabolgan (left) fights out the finish of the 2005 Hennessy Gold Cup at Newbury with L'Ami. This was Mick's comeback ride from a serious neck injury, and a very emotional day. Ironically, it was L'Ami who ended Mick's career when falling at the second fence in the 2008 Grand National.

Stormyfairweather jumps the last ahead of Fadalko on the way to a second successive victory in the Cathcart Challenge Cup Chase at the Cheltenham Festival in 2000. He was a very special horse owned by our close friends Christopher and Bridget Hanbury.

'We got him home that night, but he couldn't get up the following morning. It was awful, just awful. It's so sad when you know that horses haven't reached their potential, tough on everyone but toughest on the lad who looked after them. You just feel steamrollered. Then a couple of weeks later you uncover another potential star and everyone says that you've replaced the one you've lost. Of course you haven't, you never replace them – you've just found a different good horse.'

He plays the stoic well but it is not his default setting. Here is a man whose emotions are easily expressed, an old-school man who merits the label 'new man' for his tendency to tears. Where another trainer might greet the cameras in the winner's enclosure with a mask of nonchalant indifference, Henderson's face is often split in two, tears rolling down his face to meet the corners of the smile coming up.

'I'm a crier,' he laughs. 'I'm emotional, probably to the extent of being very emotional. Happy occasions, sad occasions, anything can get to me – everyone knows it. Josh Gifford, who I miss enormously, was probably the only one who was worse than me on that score.

'Every race matters, even if it's just a tiny novice hurdle at Plumpton. The heart's still pounding away. When I won the Gold Cup with Long Run they told me I looked exactly like a man who'd won the Gold Cup, and that's what people want you to look like.'

Natural emotions naturally expressed are his stock-in-trade. To see them at their plainest look no further than the week of the Cheltenham Festival, the week that drives him on to greater heights more than anything else, for Cheltenham is so ingrained in his psyche thanks to the actions of his father Johnny, the exploits of Fred Winter, its very public assessment of a trainer's merit. It's the light that guides him, but that light ignites the fuse that burns down exceeding short in the preceding weeks.

Visit Henderson three weeks before Cheltenham and you find a man with his nerves on the outside for all to see. It's all bark and no bite, although he mutters about having days when he'll eat anybody, before, in the next breath, explaining that age has settled him down a bit, that he's miles better than he used to be.

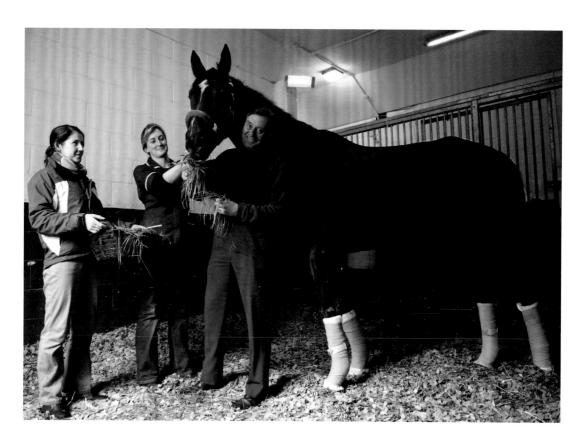

Blue is the colour, Fondmort is his name: our patient recovers at The Ridgeway Veterinary Equine Hospital after breaking his pelvis on the gallops in 2006. Here he is pictured with nurse Sarah Mason, head nurse Hannah Williams and myself. He is still in happy retirement.

'It gets a bit wild. Not just Festival week, which I get through pretty much on adrenaline alone, but the entire month leading up to it. I turn into a bit of a Cadbury's Fruit and Nut case – there's a lot of responsibility and I know there are things that will go wrong, there always are. I don't want to spend any time away from the yard at all. I want to be there where I can see everything that's going on, keep a close watch on everything. It's all about keeping your eyes and ears open for anything that might occur. And the fingers crossed.

'Our year does revolve around Cheltenham, but that applies to the whole jump season really. It all comes down to four days, those are the ones that matter.

'I am very proud of holding the record for training Cheltenham winners, even though someone will no doubt beat it one day – I'll admit to that, because Dad was so important to the place. Beating Fulke Walwyn's record of winners at the meeting meant a lot, above and beyond having seven winners there in 2012.

'Look, Fulke was a legend when I was still a schoolboy. I had a picture of Mill House on my bedroom wall where every other normal teenager would have had pictures of pretty girls. So doing anything that could be compared to him, beating records set by people like him, is very special. When it happened I felt a bit humbled.'

Which is why, for a man so amiably in thrall to his emotions and to the submerged history of the sport that he is helping to overwrite, the story of Moonlit Path is one he visits only necessarily and briefly, loath to skip it entirely but weary of its presence, wary of its impact. The facts can be pencilled lightly in – in 2009 the once-raced Moonlit Path tested positive for a banned substance, Henderson was accused and convicted of thereby trying to enhance its performance, was suspended from training for three months – but the after-effects are scored deeply and indelibly.

'I genuinely believe that it was a catastrophic misjustice. We were found guilty of trying to enhance this horse's performance – to this day I fail to understand how they could not believe, when I had the 8-13 favourite for the race, who won, and I had a six-year-old that had never seen a racecourse in its life, that was 16-1, why on earth would I want to enhance its performance? It doesn't make sense. I was trying to help the horse through its first race.

'Up until then, and since then, my record had been untainted. Now all of a sudden it's got this ghastly "thing" against it. My good name had gone. The very worst of it was that it was the Queen's horse, and I was so embarrassed to have put her into that position. Thankfully she was very supportive, and life went on.

'But it hurt, because you know whether you're guilty or innocent – and I was innocent. It's been forgotten, hasn't it?'

Racing has forgotten, or put the memory away, and moved on. Henderson has not forgotten, and won't, the fleeting loss of his good name making him poor indeed. Perhaps it served as a spur, an unconscious pricking beneath the skin that he would no doubt explain away by talking of better horses, of more horses, of the support of his trusted owners, of the vagaries of fortune's wheel that one day runs over one's toes and the next day propels one to the higher ground, for since his enforced hiatus Henderson has gone from strength to strength.

There has been almost an unending stream of brilliant young horses, a production line of aces who have elevated him to the peak of his profession. Punjabi and Binocular supplied a fourth and fifth Champion Hurdle, Long Run provided a long-awaited Gold Cup, Bobs Worth hinted at the carefully husbanded seedcorn for another, in time. And there arose the paragon that is Sprinter Sacre, a steeplechaser apparently, eerily, without flaw.

At the breathless end of the 2011–12 season he had the trainer's championship almost in his grasp – for the first time since the 1986–87 campaign – until his great rival and friend Paul Nicholls snatched it away when Neptune Collonges won the Grand National, which is still the only big race to have thus far eluded Henderson. At the time he played down the pressures of the title race, relegating it to a tertiary importance rather than a primary focus. 'The trainers' championship? No, it certainly isn't the be-all and end-all. It would be nice if it happened, but it's more important to me that I have good horses and they run well. I was champion years ago and it would be quite rare, I suppose, to regain the title after so many years – but I have a lot more to keep me awake at night without worrying about that.'

He moves on, citing the invaluable influence of former trainer Charlie Morlock, now back-up to him and Corky Browne, yet another wise head to complement the long list of assistant trainers of which so many have gone on to be successful in their own right, those youngsters who have filled and are filling the shoes once occupied all those years ago by Henderson at Fred Winter's Uplands academy. And if that sounds a little like the neat closing of a circle then Henderson himself supplies that evidence, caught as he is on the cusp between past, present and future as all the stories eventually reach their conclusion.

'Now we have a yardful of horses that can be mentioned in the same breath as those great ones at Fred's, Bula, Pendil, Lanzarote and the others. People have mentioned it before and I always find that humbling, that I've possibly come full circle in my career.

Three in a line: Punjabi and Barry (centre) give us a fourth Champion Hurdle 22 years after See You Then's third victory, getting the better of Binocular with AP McCoy (left) and Celestial Halo (Ruby Walsh) in a tight finish. Binocular won the race for us the following year.

'That's the kind of thing that can make you feel old, but I don't feel old. Mind you, I was presented with my first grandson Harry this year, and that really makes me feel old.

'I'll go on for at least another ten years, if I'm lucky enough to get them. I'm having fun, a lot of fun and I think everyone else is too. I won't say it's any less fun now than it was, of course, but back in the old days it was seriously good fun. There was David Morley, who was a truly spectacular man, Josh Gifford, David Nicholson, Fred Winter, so many others including my great friend Barry Hills, who is thankfully still with us and a mile up the road. We weren't under anything like the same scrutiny then and there was a more carefree way about it.'

There's the parting glance to the good old days, and a nod to the future as he muses about what will come after, when the seven barrows and 140 boxes of Seven Barrows have that

With my ADCs Charlie Morlock (left) and long-time head lad Corky Browne.

Keeping an eye on proceedings in the covered ride, where we start work every morning. It is probably our biggest asset because it means we can exercise the horses whatever the weather.

new curator he hinted at earlier. His daughters love the place, love their racing, but their father doubts that any of them have intentions of taking over, although he comforts himself with the words 'you never know'. It'll be a different story, and time will tell it.

And what next for Henderson himself? He pauses, looks into his glass, gives the slightly self-deprecatory answer common among trainers, the one that suggests that some higher power has as much input into the equation as any of those closer to the end that kicks and the end that bites.

'All you can ask for is a good year and healthy horses, not too many dramas, and we'll see what happens. Whatever happens, it'll be fun.'

It sounds like the beginning of another story, the last story, the best story. Armed with a pile of back numbers of the *Racing Post,* whose reports and photographs have chronicled his unbelievable season, Henderson settles back and begins to tell it…

THE EARLY MONTHS

Previous spread: Bobs Worth and Barry (number 3) clear the water jump in the 2012 Hennessy Gold Cup just behind our other runner Roberto Goldback, ridden by Jerry McGrath.

IN THE OLD DAYS we didn't get them running again until October and it's the same now really. We don't do a great deal of summer jumping – I'm not a fan of it – but if we can get 20 winners by the time the season 'proper' starts it's all runs on the board.

We always have a small team of selected jump horses who run on the Flat and are hopefully good enough to compete at the big meetings like Ascot, Goodwood and York.

The horses start coming back to us from mid-July. Charlie Vigors has around 40 summering with him at nearby Hillwood Stud, including all of Michael Buckley's. Sprinter Sacre summers with Juliet and David Minton at Mill House Stud in Much Wenlock, Shropshire, along with all of the Moulds' other horses and the Queen's.

Robert Chugg, in Worcestershire, has all of Richard Kelvin Hughes's horses which are in training, as well as his mares and their progeny. We've had so much fun putting together a high-class broodmare band, which includes My Petra and Chomba Womba, and hopefully the first of their progeny will come into training for the 2013–14 season.

There are plenty at home with their owners, including those belonging to JP McManus, Simon Munir, Robert Waley-Cohen and Dai Walters. They love having them, but eight weeks is plenty long enough for a horse – any athlete – to spend idle.

However, they do need a mental break and they can't grow while they're in training because their whole metabolism is concentrated on getting fit and staying fit. They can't do two things at once. So, the summer break is a chance for them to grow and develop, and it can be extraordinary how they change – sometimes we hardly recognise them when they come back to the yard.

I'm a notoriously late starter as we take a long time in prep. Autumn can be a dangerous time because the horses are heavier and not as fit, and if you go galloping them hard too soon you can hit problems. We don't do roadwork like we used to – it's amazing how many of the old theories have gone completely out of the window.

We do at least a month's trotting on the grass before they canter every day, which is very different from the good old days, as is the feeding which is now much more of a science. One would no more feed a bran mash to the horses these days than to the children.

One of the most important aspects of feeding is the hay, which is checked monthly by a very important and fascinating man called Alan Creighton. He also monitors the general hygiene of the yard. The wet summer was one of the biggest problems last season and this meant that Alan had to test the hay relentlessly because we were always worried about it – bad hay can destroy you.

One bit of sad news I had to report in September 2012 before we got under way was that Spirit Son, who didn't run at that year's Cheltenham Festival, would miss this season as well. His career was also in jeopardy and this is what I told the *Post* at the time:

Spirit Son sustained a tendon injury before last season's Champion Hurdle, which was a bitter blow in itself. Following treatment to repair the tendon, he went to Charlie and Tracy Vigors' Hillwood Stud.

He had been there six weeks when Charlie rang me early on a Sunday morning – I was in Glasgow airport returning from the Scottish Grand National meeting – to say they had found Spirit Son on the floor of his box and unable to get up.

Having spoken to his owner Michael Buckley I flew south and went straight to Hillwood, where Charlie and the vet, Jamie O'Gorman, had managed to get him on to a tarpaulin on the lawn in front of his box.

He was lying flat out but could move his neck and tried to get up, but his hind-end was obviously not working, although he showed none of the normal symptoms of a spinal or pelvic injury that one normally associates with paralysis.

It was impossible to know what had happened but it was important that he did not lie on one side for too long

Spirit Son and Barry winning the Mersey Novices' Hurdle at Aintree in April 2011, with Cue Card (right) back in second.

and it was necessary to turn him over approximately every two hours. He would eat the grass at his head and we picked him buckets of fresh grass and hand fed him.

The vets feared that if he did not improve by the afternoon they would have to put him to sleep. And anyway, how was he going to get through the night lying outside? It was starting to rain and get colder.

He seemed remarkably calm and Corky joined us, together with Jamie and another vet, Bruce Bladon, and Charlie's staff.

He hadn't improved but he was fighting, and having spoken to Michael – who cares about his horses more than anybody I know – he was as determined as we were that we were going to fight for him. We made several calls to identify the top intensive care expert in the country and two people suggested Celia Marr from Rossdales Veterinary Surgeons in Newmarket.

I managed to contact her while she was at a party in Newmarket and she kindly agreed to come straight down. However, it was going to take approximately three hours to get all the necessary medicinal needs together and be driven down.

As it was getting dark, the problem was how to cover him. We contacted Lambourn Marquees and within an hour or so we had erected a marquee over him together with strip lighting, deep straw and loads of fresh grass and we were still turning him over every two hours.

Celia's arrival at about 9pm was a bit like M*A*S*H descending on us as she and her intern swept in armed with equipment and carried out a multitude of tests and set up drips and fluids. She could not identify the problem but mentioned the possibility of a rare virus that attacks the neurological system.

I had to drag Corky home after midnight, leaving Celia, Charlie and the team for the night. Everybody had agreed that he must be a very brave horse, but then all very good horses are probably very brave and he was fighting very hard. Celia felt it was critical that he was up by 6 or 7am the next morning, or he probably never would be.

At 3am, Charlie texted me to say 'He's up'. We all went back to Hillwood first thing although he was back down again – he was too exhausted to stay up for long. Celia had taken lots of tests and returned to Newmarket.

Hannah Leech, who looked after him and rode him every day at Seven Barrows, joined the vigil. While still having to turn him over regularly, he eventually – but only with a lot of help and support – managed to stand up again. He was amazingly perky but obviously very weak and it was a matter of having a vigil of four people around the clock to either turn him or help him up – and back down again.

Corky, Neil, Hannah and Charlie's squad were all part of the round-the-clock team. This was obviously going to be a very long battle but Michael wanted everything possible done for him.

The tests showed he had indeed been infected by the suggested virus, which can lie dormant in any horse, and we therefore assumed this to be the case.

Although the virus seemed the logical explanation, Celia always said she would at some stage like to bone scan his neck to rule out a fracture, but this was obviously not possible until he could move. He began to get stronger and took some very wobbly steps when his hind legs did not co-ordinate with his front. He resembled somebody staggering out of a night club at 4am much the worse for wear.

Charlie had a large box padded throughout and CCTV cameras put in and Spirit Son managed to take the few necessary steps from the marquee that had been his home for five days. He was still unable to get up unassisted but he was eating and taking a few more steps each day.

Corky went over regularly to help Hannah and the team take him out for short walks, holding on to him by his tail. The progress was slow but significant, even though the prognosis was still very poor. The virus is evidently seen more in the USA and is very rare in the UK. Recovery rates are pretty low, but Spirit Son did not know the stats and he was, as everyone had continued to say, the bravest horse they had known.

He was deemed stable enough to be driven to O'Gormans on June 11 for a bone scan on his neck. The travel was no problem but the scan revealed fractures to the fifth cervical vertebra, which brought a whole new scenario to the situation. Was it the virus or the fracture, and how had he fractured it? The scan was inconclusive and a more in-depth investigation was required by means of a CT scan and myelogram, but this was going to have to be performed in Newmarket. We weren't unduly worried about the extra journey, but we were very concerned about the general anaesthetic he needed.

However, we had to try to go forward aware of the risks involved. He came through the anaesthetic but with concrete evidence of damage to the C5 and C6 vertebrae.

The poor fellow was quite shaken by this but soon returned to Hillwood, where he settled down again as we discussed the next step. There were two known surgeons who could perform an obviously extremely complicated and undoubtedly dangerous operation, one in the USA and one, John Walmsley, in Hampshire, who luckily was prepared to perform what was going to be a huge task with major risks involved. But it was the only option.

Michael, Charlie, myself, Hannah et al had to endure a long, nervous wait for the news but, once again, he pulled through when we knew the odds were unfavourable.

It was back to Hillwood a week later for eight weeks' box rest with all his food at head height. Charlie felt that even after a couple of days his whole demeanour was a little better and, amazingly, he looked remarkably bright and well.

He's now into the last three weeks of this part of the drama and then we'll be able to see if his coordination has improved.

The prognosis for racing always has been and still is very low, but he deserved a chance to have a life, whether it's on

Owner Michael Buckley with the recovering Spirit Son. Michael suffered a torrid season following the highs of the previous year with the likes of Finian's Rainbow and Mossley. He has been a great friend for a very long time, as well as being a true sportsman and National Hunt fan for many years.

Overleaf: Watching the horses pull up at the end of the Faringdon Road gallops. We use these gallops all year round and do nearly all of our fast work on grass rather than on the all-weather.

a racecourse or in another role. Michael has been incredible to support this venture throughout, while Charlie, Tracy and the team at Hillwood have been quite amazing and we wouldn't be anywhere near where we are now without them. Hannah, Corky and many others have played their part, while Celia Marr, John Walmsley and O'Gormans have provided the veterinary expertise and have all been outstanding.

With them, and not to mention Spirit Son's strength and will, we still have a dream.

It has been a staggering story of human and equine determination, and whatever the outcome I cannot possibly express how incredible everybody has been in this fight.

We built this all-weather gallop in 1994 and it has been invaluable to us. The views are spectacular and are made even better when you see Sprinter Sacre and Nico de Boinville work. Sprinter is pure class just doing this.

Casting my eye over first lot in the autumn sunshine. The gallop starts in Berkshire and ends in Oxfordshire.

I'm watching you, Mr Whitaker! Simonsig, with Holly Conte on board, spots the Racing Post's *photographer.*

To see the horse sound and happy is the only reward and, if it did happen, the word 'miracle' would not be far away.

Unfortunately, Spirit Son is not going to race again. We have sadly had to accept he is never going to make the racecourse. It is down to Michael's perseverance and to Charlie's care that he at least gets his retirement. The plan is for him to relocate to the wonderful institution that is Greatwood, a charity which rehabilitates and rehomes former racehorses.

Meanwhile, away from the drama of Spirit Son the stable routine continued.

Plans for the horses start to be made as they come back to us, although some schedules are easier to set out than others. It's fun for everyone, sitting down over a nice meal and a bottle of wine and mapping out the future for the top horses. For example, Ronnie Bartlett and I must have discussed a hundred times whether Simonsig was going to stay over hurdles or switch to fences – without ever coming to a firm conclusion.

In the end, with Binocular, Darlan and Grandouet around, we thought it would probably be better if Simonsig got on with it and started jumping fences. Sprinter Sacre was quite simple: we knew he would start off in the Tingle Creek. We thought about going chasing with Oscar Whisky, but Dai Walters was keen to stay over hurdles.

The plan was always for Bobs Worth to start off in the Hennessy; he wasn't going to be a King George horse, whereas Long Run had the King George as his main objective and the Betfair Chase was the right race to take him on to Kempton.

We had previously gone the Hennessy route with Trabolgan, who had also won the RSA Chase. It's a good race for the second-season novice to take on the seniors for the first time. I always say I don't think I could run Bobs Worth more than twice a year anyway, because I don't think his owners could take the excitement.

With plans for the horses mapped out it was time for the season to really get going. Before the Hennessy, Rodney Masters talked to our current stable jockey Barry Geraghty about life at Seven Barrows and the horses he was looking forward to riding:

Barry and Riverside Theatre (left) are behind Albertas Run and AP, but come out on top in the Ryanair Chase at Cheltenham in 2012. This was undoubtedly one of the greatest rides of all time by Barry.

8.45am. Nicky Henderson's kitchen at Seven Barrows. After a wet first lot, Barry Geraghty and Tony McCoy are toasting their bodies alongside the Aga at full roar. Between them, Sophie shuffles the pots and pans of a full breakfast. Seeing the two jockeys together, thoughts drift to Riverside Theatre, Wichita Lineman and their Cheltenham Festival wins. Two of the most stunning mind-over-matter rides of our generation.

As his was the most recent, the skilfully articulate Geraghty is persuaded to give a reprise of Riverside Theatre's Ryanair Chase win. We are immediately riding with him. 'He was cautious at the second. From then on I was on the back foot. He raced behind the bridle. He was getting in a bit tight and losing momentum. He wasn't actually making mistakes, just catching the top. Captain Chris was jumping right, into us, at several fences. If it hadn't been for Sam Twiston-Davies allowing me room on the inner down the back I doubt we'd have got there. Approaching the fourth-last it looked far from promising. But I knew there was plenty left. I threw him at the fence and he responded. I got greedy and did the same at the next. Suddenly we were in a position where we could win. He slogged it out from there. All credit to a brave horse.'

Barry rides Roberto Goldback to win the United House Gold Cup at Ascot in November 2012 – second leg of a notable double for owner Simon Munir, whose Une Artiste had won a valuable mares' hurdle at Wetherby earlier that afternoon. Simon has been a great supporter of ours, but I'm not sure whether we come before or after his beloved Arsenal. Whenever he takes me to the Emirates we often take AP, who is waiting to take over from Arsene Wenger!

He does not regard that as his most accomplished ride. 'A good ride is when you have options and you select all the right ones. I suppose the ride I put a lot into, mentally, was Punjabi's Champion Hurdle. I was anxious to stay as close to the leaders as possible without putting him under pressure. I didn't want to take them on too soon, and most definitely not Celestial Halo. We led at the last and then held him by a neck.'

By now, the sturdily built Geraghty is tucking into his breakfast, with double most everything on his plate.

Yet he can ride at 10st 1lb when required, credit for which he directs entirely to his wife Paula, who is a nutritionist by profession. 'Paula has my metabolism in terrific shape and that's why I can eat like this. I'm able to burn it off. In the 24 hours before the Paddy Power I ran 7km and 8km on the treadmill at Oaksey House.'

When Geraghty is in Britain he lodges in five-star luxury at what he portrays as the Lambourn branch of Sandy Lane: the home of Henderson's assistant trainer Ben Pauling and his fiancée Sophie Finch. They spoil him rotten and he revels in it. No doubt his bed is turned down at 7pm with a chocolate left on a pillow.

Come the eve of 2100 when turf historians review the first decades of the past century they may analyse why the two pre-eminent trainers retained stable jockeys who lived in another country. They will evaluate the results and conclude the thumping success of the arrangement. Apart from the obvious skills of the jockeys, perhaps it is healthy for a trainer–jockey relationship to have a built-in breathing space. In addition, there is an invaluable incentive for the stable's other jockeys that opportunities will always be available.

Geraghty finds the commute easy enough. He has ridden in the 3.15 at Kempton yet been home by 5.45pm to read a bedtime story to his daughters Siofra, aged seven, and Orla, 18 months.

Seated alongside him on many flights is Ruby Walsh. Their chatter has not touched on Saturday week's Sandown showdown between Sprinter Sacre and Sanctuaire and is unlikely to do so. 'We have a similar sense of humour and get on great together,' Geraghty says. 'I know there's no point winding him up about a race because he'd just laugh, and vice versa.'

Geraghty's association with Henderson dates from the 1999–2000 season. His first ride for the stable was on Geos, who carried 9st 12lb into second in The Ladbroke at Leopardstown. One of their early big-race wins together came with Isio in Newbury's 2004 Vodafone Gold Cup.

He says he can appreciate why Henderson finds it frightening to watch Sprinter Sacre. 'I'd much the same feeling when he ran at Doncaster in his first novice chase because I was watching on the big screen at Cheltenham. But he's not frightening to ride. Although he wants to get on with things he's never out of control because he has such a good mouth and is well mannered. He'll come up for you at a fence. He's so athletic, with such a spring in his stride, that I call him Usain Bolt. He's a monster.'

Geraghty cannot believe his luck at the treasure chest open to him.

'Simonsig has so much class that I had to take a pull coming out of the back at Aintree and that rarely happens at that level. His schooling over fences is going well. Oscar Whisky is an outstanding talent. He wobbled badly after the World Hurdle but that he won a few weeks later at Aintree was a tribute

Isio provided Barry and myself with one of our first big-race successes together in the Vodafone Gold Cup at Newbury in March 2004. Isio had previously won the Victor Chandler Chase in one of the best chases I can remember when he beat Azertyuiop by a neck. He was owned by Peter and Louise Gibbings, who have had horses with us for a long time and still do.

to his courage and also the trainer's immense skills. Finian's Rainbow hated the Ascot ground but is right up there with the best and he'll be back. Grandouet will be a big player in the Champion Hurdle. I've ridden him a fair bit at home recently and I believe he has improved again.'

Two decades ago most jump jockeys were retired by 32, whether through injury or choice. Now 40 would be a more feasible cut-off point for those with the option, despite the fact substantially more rides are taken each year by most jockeys. That is counterbalanced by higher degrees of fitness and dietary control, as well as improved body protectors and skullcaps.

Geraghty is 33. 'I love my job so much I'd like to keep going until I'm 50,' he grins. Folly or achievable? For a reaction to that utterance we both look across to McCoy, still in the

*Previous spread: With
Sprinter Sacre – and Maybe
the labrador. She was once
quite well trained, but now
people who visit us at Seven
Barrows must hope I train
my horses better than I
trained her!*

NEWBURY

DECEMBER 1, 2012

Hennessy Gold Cup Chase
3m 2½f

1 Bobs Worth   4-1f
Barry Geraghty

2 Tidal Bay   8-1
Ruby Walsh

3 First Lieutenant   12-1
Bryan Cooper

4 The Package   8-1
Tom Scudamore

Distances 3¼l, 5l, 6l

kitchen, but on the far side with his head buried in newspapers.
He would beat Geraghty to the half-century by five years.
The champion possibly didn't hear us, but there was just a
trace of a wry smile. But then again, perhaps it was something
he'd just read.

**Bobs Worth gave us a memorable second Hennessy
victory after Trabolgan in 2005 and his great bunch of
owners a marvellous thrill at Newbury on the first day
of December. Lee Mottershead reported for the *Post*:**

If a spark were needed to set light to Nicky Henderson's
season, it came on the perfect stage, in the perfect race and
with the perfect horse, an animal who looked on paper to be
a textbook Hennessy hero and now has bookmakers believing
him to be the likeliest winner of the Betfred Cheltenham
Gold Cup.

The winter had not begun badly for the master of Seven
Barrows but it had started much better for Paul Nicholls.
While many have long regarded a Henderson championship
triumph as a *fait accompli*, recent results had triggered a
concertinaing of the title rivals' odds.

It was to Ditcheat that the Paddy Power Gold Cup and
Betfair Chase victors [Al Ferof and Silviniaco Conti] returned,
but it was in Lambourn that the 2012 Hennessy Gold Cup
victor last night went to bed after Bobs Worth brushed aside
the Nicholls-trained Tidal Bay for a triumph that earned loud
and hearty approval from the Newbury faithful.

Just seven days earlier Henderson had seen his first ever
Gold Cup winner Long Run beaten at Haydock by Nicholls'
bright young hope Silviniaco Conti. On a crisp, clear afternoon
at Henderson's local track, Bobs Worth confirmed himself to
be a hope every bit as bright.

Bobs Worth, a no-nonsense, far-from-flashy chaser sold
to Henderson in May 2009 by Barry Geraghty, is now as
short as 7-2 favourite for the Gold Cup, Paddy Power's quote
being only a point and a half less than the best available 5-1.
Such odds reflect not only the winner's seriously progressive
profile but also his unblemished four-from-four record at
Cheltenham, where he will return seeking a third consecutive

Festival strike following wins in the Albert Bartlett Novices'
Hurdle and RSA Chase.

With a crack at the William Hill King George VI Chase
all but ruled out, it is also expected to be Cheltenham that
Bobs Worth visits for his Gold Cup trial, with the Argento
Chase suggested by Malcolm Kimmins, head of the jubilant
Not Afraid Partnership, as the intended next stop.

Yesterday Bobs Worth started 4-1 favourite and defeated
top-weight Tidal Bay by three and a quarter lengths after
taking the lead approaching the final fence. Fancied opponents
First Lieutenant and The Package were ultimately soundly
beaten back in third and fourth.

Henderson, who only this week believed Bobs Worth had
bloomed, said: 'He was the young pretender and if he is going
to make it to the top he probably did have to win. Even so, it's
mighty nice that he has done.

'Earlier in the season I wasn't happy with him, but three
nights ago I looked at him at evening stables and thought,
"Hello!" It was like watching a rose come out. All of a sudden
he looked fit, healthy and really well. That was the first the
time I thought he had a chance of winning.'

He added: 'He is an adorable character. All he wants to do is
please you. He isn't a Sprinter Sacre, who wants to show off. He
just hunts around without ever really being hard on the bridle.

'You would never notice him in the middle of a race
and you wouldn't notice him on the gallops, but then at the
second last you suddenly see Bob. He is very special.'

He also came at the special price of £20,000 when bought
by Henderson at Doncaster from Geraghty, who had paid
€16,500 for the son of Bob Back two and a half years earlier.

Kimmins, a former Newbury steward and director whose
five-strong syndicate ultimately settled the bill, described
himself as 'blown away'.

Geraghty felt the same, saying: 'I've known this horse since
he was a yearling and to win a race like this means everything
to me. It has given me as big a thrill as winning any other race.

'This horse gives everything and he has the quality to
match. His profile ticks all the boxes for the Gold Cup. He
is game, he loves it and he is great fun. He is what racing is
all about.'

And Alastair Down was on hand to describe a Hennessy victory that took high rank in the history of the great race:

It's the total absence of flash that makes you warm to Bobs Worth – he doesn't do spectacular, there is nothing glitzy about him and he is not one of those types who takes the breath away.

But he was an utterly clear-cut winner of yesterday's Hennessy and he has all the attributes you look for in a long-distance chaser – solid jumping leavened with plenty of stamina and more than once he has shown that he can dig deep and battle.

So he is both a stayer and a scrapper but, in all fairness, as Bobs Worth now has two Festival wins and a Hennessy on his sideboard he can hardly be devoid of at least a smattering of class as well.

And Bobs Worth now sets off on a hard road to Cheltenham that has been successfully negotiated before although not with any great frequency. In the last 40 years only two Hennessy winners, Bregawn in 1982 and Denman in 2007, have gone on to win the Gold Cup the same season.

Another who should have done the double was Jodami, whose narrow defeat in 1992 by Sibton Abbey from 21lb out of the weights remains the single most inexplicable result of a top-class chase in my lifetime. And my lasting bafflement does not begin to match that of his trainer Peter Beaumont who still shakes his head from side to side in resigned and rueful astonishment.

Bobs Worth was the beneficiary of a masterfully patient stalk of a ride from his former owner Barry Geraghty, who just bided his time and could be seen going conspicuously well toward the inner with fully six to jump.

All the way up the straight it looked just a matter of when Geraghty would play him and Bobs Worth led going to the last. Although Ruby Walsh had shepherded the rejuvenated Tidal Bay into a challenging position he could never rattle Geraghty's cage and the winner strode home purposefully to win by three and a quarter lengths, which were value for a couple more. Back in third, First Lieutenant gave his all and emerged with huge credit – he has another major race in him this season.

In the winner's enclosure after the Hennessy we had a rare sighting of Corky (to the right of me) on a racecourse. Newbury and Cheltenham are usually the only tracks he goes to. The notion that Bobs Worth is not very big is shown to be incorrect. You can see here that Tomas Dolezal, who looks after him, is very tall and obviously not a rider!

When Denman became the last RSA winner to come on here and win the Hennessy it was an earthquake of a performance that left you feeling the aftershocks for days. Humping 11st 12lb and ripping his field apart, you knew you had just witnessed something eruptive that had changed the chasing weather.

There were no pyrotechnics from Bobs Worth because he is not that type, but make no mistake, this performance was mined from a very similar seam to that of Denman. Bobs Worth won this off a mark of 160, just 1lb less than Paul Nicholls' bruiser, and that puts him smack in the Gold Cup mix.

What's more, he has already won twice at the Festival and is in the hands of a man who all but took the course home in his pocket last March. Henderson treated the press pack to some splendid stuff about walking into Bobs Worth's box on Wednesday evening and the horse striking him 'as a rose that had suddenly come into flower'.

It may sound like an early pitch from Nicky to be the next poet laureate but actually it is very revealing of Henderson's modus operandi and speaks volumes about him.

He doesn't pretend to be one of the 21st century's towering intellectuals but he brings something to the feast that is far more useful than brains, which are two a penny.

Nicky is one of those trainers who can sense things about his horses, he can sniff the breeze and feel a change in the way the wind is blowing.

He has what only the very top flight have – a genuine instinct for how their horses are and particularly when they have, unseen by other eyes, suddenly turned a corner.

Henderson is rightly going to bypass the King George and will probably take Bobs Worth back to Cheltenham for Trials Day at the end of January. He describes his Hennessy winner as 'a thorough professional who loves his work'. Only a lunatic would ask for more.

So Bobs Worth now rises to the top of the ante-post pile for our greatest chase. But it could be all change again in the market after Flemenstar and Sir Des Champs clash in the John Durkan Chase at Punchestown next Sunday, a confrontation that has all Ireland agog. They are two chasers of boundless potential – Flemenstar for the minnows and Sir Des Champs, already a dual Festival winner like Bobs Worth, representing the big battalions.

And 24 hours before that clash we have Sprinter Sacre versus Sanctuaire in a two-miler that would put the tingle in any creek.

Dull old game this jump racing! It'll never catch on.

Sprinter Sacre was ready for his reappearance in the Tingle Creek, although in the days leading up to Sandown I did admit to being absolutely petrified at the prospect.

However, it could have been someone else worrying about him. For one thing, we were sent Sprinter Sacre out of Raymond Mould's job-lot that he purchased from Minty. He could so easily have gone to another trainer, because we were simply sent three horses, I didn't pick them out. We also got Charles Onze and Semi Colon, who aren't quite in the same league as Sprinter Sacre.

For another, we'd seen Sprinter Sacre as a foal. Several of us had gone to deepest France where they have a show – not a sale – with lots of different classes… mares with foals, yearlings, two-year-olds, you name it. And if we'd been on

With Long Run – having a laugh on a press day for the King George VI Chase.

the ball we could have bought Sprinter Sacre as a foal and Quevega as a three-year-old – ten grand might have bought them both.

We may have missed out on the five-time Cheltenham Festival-winning mare, but at least we got Sprinter Sacre in the end. And at Sandown I need not have worried as Sprinter got his season off to a flying start in the Tingle Creek, as Jon Lees reported:

Nicky Henderson had spent the week being petrified by the prospect of putting Sprinter Sacre through the stiffest test of his career, but the only ones who should be in fear are the rivals who dare to take him on after the champion chaser-elect produced an imperious comeback display yesterday.

Sprinter Sacre and Barry jump the first in the Tingle Creek, the first fence of an amazing year. We were all nervous beforehand as usual and owner Caroline Mould is no better than me! I know how much she cares about Sprinter and he is very much her horse.

Sprinter Sacre and Sanctuaire went into the Sportingbet Tingle Creek Chase separated by only 3lb on BHA figures but in reality the gulf in class was huge, as last season's Racing Post Arkle Chase winner handed out a thorough beating to Paul Nicholls' best ever novice chaser.

The nearest thing jump racing has to Frankel, now that Kauto Star is in retirement, coasted over the line 15 lengths clear of Kumbeshwar, with a tired Sanctuaire third, to win with his head in his chest.

In so doing he stretched his unbeaten run over fences to six in front of an elated crowd of 11,100, but not before Sprinter Sacre had been asked searching questions by Ruby Walsh on Sanctuaire.

At the track where Sanctuaire had taken the Celebration Chase by 17 lengths, Walsh set out to make all the running.

Sportingbet Tingle
Creek Chase 2m

1 Sprinter Sacre 4-11f
Barry Geraghty

2 Kumbeshwar 25-1
Wayne Hutchinson

3 Sanctuaire 11-4
Ruby Walsh

Distances 15l, 4½l

At one point they held an eight-length advantage, but Sprinter Sacre and Barry Geraghty gradually made up the deficit and, by the time they reached the Pond fence, victory was assured for Caroline Mould's champion.

'He has certainly got the wow factor,' said Henderson. 'It's been a long summer and long autumn waiting for this. We knew there was going to be a head-to-head and I've got to admit I've been petrified about Sanctuaire.

'That pace was going to stretch anybody and even Barry said it was only when he got to the Pond fence he got back into his comfort zone. Barry said the ground was as soft as he would ever want to go on, but he's just class.

'When you know something is a bit special you just want it to stay that way and anything bar a good performance was going to be disappointing. The people who came here were going to be disappointed if they didn't see something special from one of the two. We hoped it would be our one and it was.

'That's as good two-mile chasing as you will see.'

Geraghty admitted it was not entirely straightforward, saying: 'It's the first time I've had to work early but going into the Railway fences I had Ruby well covered. They went a proper gallop and it rode like a really good race.

'He was faultless. It's very rare you see a horse as good-looking as that be as good as he is. He's like Concorde.'

Even-money across the board for the Sportingbet Queen Mother Champion Chase before racing yesterday, Sprinter Sacre was offered by Boylesports at a standout 4-7 after racing, but he was available only at between 1-2 and 2-5 with rival firms, with Sizing Europe and Finian's Rainbow both on 8-1.

Sanctuaire is still in the Champion Chase betting but trainer Paul Nicholls did not sound keen on a rematch. 'He's run a nice enough race and we had to give it a try, but what's happened is what everyone expected to happen,' he said.

'He got tired but he just wasn't good enough – it's as simple as that.'

Newly crowned Racing Writer of the Year Alastair Down was awed by Sprinter's stupendous success:

Top-class two-mile chasers pell-melling it around Sandown is the very stuff of exhilaration, but Sprinter Sacre elevated the experience to a new summit yesterday with a Tingle Creek victory that was nothing short of revelatory.

The old adage has it that 'power corrupts and absolute power corrupts absolutely' – well the power of this horse excites, and it excites absolutely.

There is something exuberant and spectacular about Sprinter Sacre at full tilt that borders on the breathtaking and he threw in some leaps here that the word extravagant cannot get close to describing.

From the time Sanctuaire led Sprinter Sacre over the first and they headed up to the anticipatory stands, battle was joined and you forgot about the other runners as every sense focused on the big two. Going into the back straight Ruby Walsh and Sanctuaire were six lengths clear, and when that lead stretched to the best part of ten down the searching seven-fence examination of Sandown's far side the eye kept being drawn to the favourite, looking for some tell-tale sign of unease from Barry Geraghty.

But Geraghty didn't have even the suggestion of a bother on him.

When he asked Sprinter Sacre, who had made just one half-error at the fourth, to close down Sanctuaire it was done with an almost imperceptible surge of power that took them up to their rival seemingly without effort. That was the extraordinary thing about this performance: at one minute Sprinter Scare had plenty of lengths to find and yet, just a glance later, that job was done and he was steaming into the lead going to the Pond fence and still on the bridle.

From then on it became a rout as Sprinter Sacre sauntered clear and, perfect over the last two with Geraghty keeping the big horse's mind on the job, he won by 15 lengths from Kumbeshwar, who overhauled an understandably tired Sanctuaire after the final fence.

The last time we saw a two-mile chase performance of this enormity was Master Minded's 19-length evisceration of Voy Por Ustedes in the 2008 Champion Chase, when the Paul Nicholls-trained chaser scaled heights he was never quite to conquer again, superb though he was. I well recall the thrill

Panic over: Barry returns to the winner's enclosure on Sprinter Sacre after the Tingle Creek. I don't know what all the fuss was about!

of that Cheltenham afternoon and the sense of unrestrained excitement that only exceptional horses bring with them – and then only rarely.

But at Sandown yesterday we surely saw a performance of a very similar stripe. You can certainly argue that Sanctuaire performed below expectations – a splendidly straightforward Nicholls said, 'He wasn't good enough, it's as simple as that' – and beating the gritty Kumbeshwar 15 lengths ain't going to set the River Lambourn on fire of itself, but I thought the winner was nothing short of astonishing.

The race was run in a six-second quicker time than that set by the mightily promising Captain Conan – a magnificent brick-shelter of a beast – in the novice chase and my Channel 4 colleague Jim McGrath said that if you equated that to about 30 lengths on the prevailing ground no sensible judge would want to start an argument.

Captain Conan and Barry put in a mighty leap on their way to winning the Henry VIII Novices' Chase at Sandown Park. This was the first of three Grade 1 novice chase victories for him in the 2012–13 season. He runs in the colours of the Triermore Stud, which is Christopher and Bridget Hanbury's family home in Ireland.

And what kept springing to the front of the brain was the overwhelming impression that never for one second was Sprinter Sacre out of his comfort zone. It was all about power to spare, rather like those truly hair-raising high-performance cars that have their top speed limited to 170mph in case they take off into orbit. The two-mile world lies at his feet.

And if Sprinter Sacre was all about brilliance and the majesty of pure class, this wonderful afternoon brought us some fabulous action from jumping's boiler room with the victory of the 14-year-old Hello Bud over the big fences of Aintree's Becher Chase.

You will race for many a year and stand witness through many a frozen winter afternoon before you see anything as plain old-fashioned emotional and heart-warming as watching Hello Bud repelling all boarders up that brute of an Aintree run-in.

I should think he was roared home from hundreds of thousands of throats across the land as he stuck out his neck and refused to stop fighting.

Oscar Whisky wins the Relkeel Hurdle at Cheltenham in December with Barry on board. His owner Dai Walters has been a fabulous supporter of National Hunt racing, and Oscar Whisky has been the flagship of his string, most of whom are raised and educated at his home near Cardiff. And, of course, Ffos Las racecourse was his inspiration. He is a larger-than-life character.

And Sam Twiston-Davies, enjoying a day of days with three winners for his dad at a course they both adore, was superb after the win, saying: 'How big is his heart? I cannot begin to explain how much this horse means to me – I was nearly crying up the run-in.'

Well I don't care how wet and weedy it may be but, 200 miles south, I was struggling in a similar state watching an old warrior put in the sort of raw effort and sheer guts that make jump racing what it is.

So this was a special afternoon that brought us the best of what we love most in the sport. Sprinter Sacre is a shining light who may be capable of true greatness and is already far above the foothills of that ambition. And at more than twice his age, the likes of Hello Bud can still reach out and tap you on the shoulder to remind you there is something about a steeplechaser's big-hearted appetite for a battle that has the capacity to move mountains.

The season was beginning to take shape, with Sprinter Sacre winning and Long Run finishing second to Silviniaco Conti in the Betfair Chase at Haydock, and next up was Simonsig. I had been very happy with his schooling prior to his much-anticipated chasing debut at Ascot the Friday before Christmas. Happily, everything went according to plan, as Graham Dench reported:

ASCOT

DECEMBER 21, 2012

Betfred Novices' Chase
2m3f

1 Simonsig   2-9f
Barry Geraghty

2 Sulpius   25-1
Jamie Moore

Distance 49l

The chasing debut Nicky Henderson had been dreading passed without incident for 2-9 chance Simonsig, and after a 49-length defeat of just one other finisher in the Grade 2 Betfred Novices' Chase the grey is as short as 6-4 favourite to emulate stablemate Sprinter Sacre by winning the Racing Post Arkle Chase.

In the short term there is a chance he will make a quick return to the track in Thursday's Wayward Lad Novices' Chase at Kempton, as he barely broke sweat in a race in which Barry Geraghty was able to enjoy an armchair ride after three of the five runners were gone by halfway.

Henderson said: 'I put him in the Wayward Lad while Barry was in the office this morning and said to him it was just in case he fell off on the way to the start. He just had a jolly good school there – he hasn't had a horserace – and although I'm not ruling it in, I'm not ruling it out.'

He added: 'I'd been dreading this and it's pure relief now. He came out of last year categorically the best novice hurdler and you could easily have seen him being a Champion Hurdle horse, but Barry was keen to jump a fence.'

Geraghty has a healthy respect for Champion Hurdle second Overturn as an Arkle rival, but he was just as delighted as the trainer and said: 'We didn't go very quick but he settled well and jumped nicely. He got the revs up once or twice, but every time I got him back. You couldn't ask any more of a novice and he was foot perfect when I let him go over the last two.'

Opposite: Simonsig impresses during his winning chasing debut at Ascot with Barry on board. No-one will ever know what would have happened had we gone down the Champion Hurdle route with this fellow.

3

CHRISTMAS CRACKERS

Previous spread: Long Run and Sam Waley-Cohen (far side) eventually get up in a driving finish to the King George from Captain Chris (Richard Johnson). As you can see, Long Run's face is notably cleaner than Captain Chris's. We had been in front from quite a long way out and the ground was very soft that day. Long Run and Sam were incredibly brave to win.

CHRISTMAS TIME IS very much the same as the rest of the season. It is fun, though, as everyone is here, but obviously they can't have a usual Christmas Day because the show goes on and no one can afford to forget about the next day. Half of the staff have Christmas Day off and the other half have New Year's Day off, but a lot of them come in when they're off to ride their horses. The highlight of this Christmas was Long Run's second victory in the King George at Kempton, as Jon Lees reported:

Long Run, who seemed destined for greatness 21 months ago only to be shoved off course by a rejuvenated Kauto Star last season, scrambled his way back on to the right path with a last-gasp King George victory that proved restorative for the credibility of the horse and amateur rider Sam Waley-Cohen.

Only one victory to Long Run's name since his reputation defining Cheltenham Gold Cup triumph over twin greats Denman and Kauto Star in March 2011, and just two under rules for his part-time jockey, had raised doubts about the partnership's long-term effectiveness.

Yet on a miserably wet day at Kempton, the first for seven years in which Kauto Star was not a competitor, both horse and jockey took on their critics and emerged victorious, fighting back when their chance appeared lost at the final fence to win an attritional duel with Captain Chris to clinch their second triumph.

Long Run was prominent virtually throughout and was in front and looked in control from three fences out, but a mistake at the second-last handed an opportunity for Captain Chris to get back on terms.

Captain Chris produced a better jump at the last but Waley-Cohen summoned a final effort out of Long Run and snatched victory by a neck, with Grands Crus third and long-time leader Champion Court fourth.

KEMPTON PARK

DECEMBER 26, 2012

William Hill King
George VI Chase 3m

1 Long Run   15-8f
Mr Sam Waley-Cohen

2 Captain Chris   16-1
Richard Johnson

3 Grands Crus   7-1
Tom Scudamore

Distances nk, 14l

*Robert Waley-Cohen: a very
proud owner and dad. He is
a huge supporter of National
Hunt racing and breeding.*

'We've always believed in him and kept the faith in him,'
said Waley-Cohen. 'People have pointed at things he has done
at Haydock and at Cheltenham and said that's the end of him.

'Today was all about guts and he has a lot of them. What he
did was just spectacular and the courage he showed to get back
up again was truly wonderful.

'I think when he got to the front he pricked his ears.
Once they do that on ground like this it's hard to get them
going again. I could feel him rallying but I didn't know if the
finish line was going to come too early. I was screaming and
pushing and hoping, and he got there.'

Waley-Cohen added: 'You are as good as your last ride
in this game and the critics are as kind as the results.

'A lot of critics sit from a position of hindsight and a
position from where they don't risk very much and judge
people that are risking everything in what they do. You listen
to the critics you respect and try to give them the respect they
deserve, for better or worse.

'I listen to the people that are closest to me who analyse
the race. When you don't do things right you listen and hope
to learn. Where you feel it's not quite fair you try to brush it
under the carpet.'

The highlight of one of four wins on the card for
trainer Nicky Henderson helped cut Paul Nicholls' lead in the
trainers' championship by nearly half the £350,000 before racing,
as well as re-establish Long Run's credentials for the Gold Cup,
for which he was cut to 6-1 (from 8) by sponsor Betfred.

'Both horse and jockey have put any doubters to
rest,' said Henderson. 'Long Run has proved stamina,
willingness, guts, determination, and Sam has given him
a great ride as well.

'Between the two of them you couldn't fault it. It was
hard work today but that's hard-work ground. There were
two rather untidy jumps towards the end which looked as
though they might have been a bit expensive, but ultimately
that little extra at the end was enough to get him in front.'

Owner Robert Waley-Cohen said: 'To everyone who said
the horse wasn't winning because Sam wasn't riding it properly
we can say, "I don't think so". I just think Long Run was
slightly not 100 per cent last year.

'This wasn't at all his last chance. I thought his chance had gone when he made that rather tired mistake at the last and to rally like that you need a fit, good jockey who can stimulate a horse and a brave horse to respond; full credit to them both for getting up.'

Thirty-five minutes before the King George, Darlan had put up a superb performance to win the Christmas Hurdle, as Lee Mottershead reported:

KEMPTON PARK

DECEMBER 26, 2012

Williamhill.com
Christmas Hurdle 2m

1 Darlan   3-1
AP McCoy

2 Raya Star   8-1
Robert Thornton

3 Dodging Bullets   8-1
Ruby Walsh

Distances 4½l, 2¾l

According to Nicky Henderson, Darlan would prefer fences to hurdles, a test of stamina to one of speed, and ground considerably quicker than that he faced yesterday.

No wonder then the trainer and bookmakers were deeply impressed by his authoritative victory in a Christmas Hurdle that turned into a muddy sprint.

For the last two seasons it had been Binocular who landed the pre-King George highlight for Henderson, Tony McCoy and JP McManus.

Binocular still resides at Seven Barrows and remains on course for the Stan James Champion Hurdle, but in the affections of connections Darlan has risen to a status commensurate after powering four and a half lengths clear of upgraded handicapper Raya Star.

Dodging Bullets and 6-4 favourite Countrywide Flame filled the next two places, with Darlan's Supreme Novices' Hurdle conqueror Cinders And Ashes one place further back.

Former Champion Hurdle winner Punjabi set just a dawdling gallop and among those least suited by that was Darlan, but on a seasonal debut that had been delayed due to deep winter ground, he excelled.

'Even I was impressed,' said Henderson. 'I've always thought a lot of him but it was a funny old race. They had a sprint, which you wouldn't have guessed was exactly what Darlan wanted, but he does have speed.

'He has also always been a chaser in the making, so the hardest decision was to stay over hurdles for another year.

'We had to break cover today as one cannot see this weather changing. It's been the same for six weeks and I can see it being the same for another six weeks. He was fit

AP drives Darlan to victory in the Christmas Hurdle at Kempton. This was undoubtedly the day Darlan showed he was a genuine Champion Hurdle contender. Sadly, we will never know, but I know what JP, AP and I all thought of him.

enough but you didn't have to be that fit today as it turned into a five-furlong race.'

For most of those five furlongs, McCoy had little reason to worry.

'He was visually very impressive and he felt very impressive,' he said.

'He quickened up and on the whole he jumped well. He doesn't have the technique of Binocular but not many horses have.

'Binocular is a very exciting horse but he has had so many problems. It's the same every year.

'He only came back into training a month ago because he was so wrong after the Champion Hurdle.

'I'll do what the boss tells me but I'm sure the boss was impressed.'

Alastair Down was on hand to describe a brave victory for horse and jockey in the King George:

Long Run with Sam and myself after the King George. This second win in the race was a major triumph for them, having lost out in a great finish to the magnificent Kauto Star the previous year.

Long Run landed an attritional King George yesterday, digging down to bare rock to rally from the last and grind down Captain Chris close home in a finish that may not have been pretty but lacked nothing for sheer dour, dogged determination.

Frankly, Long Run looked cooked twice in the race. First when rooting the fifth fence from home in a juddering error that would have dislodged many jockeys, and then again when Captain Chris put in a huge leap at the last to leave Long Run a length and a half down – if not out – and it says masses about the winner's grit and durability that he found the resources to pull this one out of the embers.

Like two groggy heavyweights punching themselves almost to standstill in the 15th and final round, Captain Chris and Long Run traded blows all the way up the run-in, with Sam Waley-Cohen getting every answer in the affirmative from the winner who, rising eight next week, now has two King Georges and a Cheltenham Gold Cup in his locker.

This was just as important an afternoon for Waley-Cohen as it was for Long Run, who was on something of a mission to re-establish himself after just one win from five runs since his 2011 Gold Cup win. Two successes at the track yesterday doubled Waley-Cohen's winning tally for this season and last and, while he may not race-ride with anything like the frequency of his professional rivals, his fitness and strength were seen to good advantage from the last against the ferocious bundle of energy that is Richard Johnson.

Johnson and Captain Chris came from miles back and were still somewhere near Hampton Court with six to jump, but they picked off the non-stayers and those floundering in the ground to challenge at exactly the right moment. I thought it was a terrific ride, but the stewards deemed otherwise and handed Johnson a nine-day whip ban and fined him his £900 share of second-place prize-money. He won't like either but he will moan more about the money than the holiday!

Among the beaten horses, Champion Court ran a fine race pinging away up front, but he didn't get home and looks Ryanair bound. That race will probably also be the target for Cue Card, who was another to hit the wall. The Giant Bolster simply ran no sort of race and for some reason didn't want to know.

For all that this was a faith-affirming afternoon for Long Run's connections, you can still trade at 7-1 about him winning another Gold Cup. Long Run may be admirable in the attitude department, but all last season he looked a grinder pure and simple and that is exactly what he had to be here.

If it comes up genuinely soft at Cheltenham – and we'll need Mediterranean temperatures from now until Champion Hurdle day for it to be otherwise – then Long Run is a player, but otherwise there will always be one or two with that bit more foot.

Far away from the fleshpots of Kempton yesterday there was a special bit of Christmas cheer when Carruthers returned to form with victory at Ffos Las, carrying many a good wish and the talented Nico de Boinville, whose 7lb allowance increasingly looks the biggest piece of robbery

Overleaf: Rajdhani Express clears the final fence on the first circuit in the novice handicap chase before setting up a spectacular King George day for the Waley-Cohen family. This was the first time he showed us what a really good horse he is.

on horseback since Dick Turpin went to the bad and took the Great North Road.

Simonsig rounded off a fabulous Christmas for us with victory on the second day of the meeting. Lee Mottershead reported:

KEMPTON PARK

DECEMBER 27, 2012

Williamhill.com Wayward Lad Novices' Chase 2m

1 Simonsig   1-6f
Barry Geraghty

2 Hinterland   4-1
Ruby Walsh

3 Wings Of Smoke   16-1
Michael Byrne

Distances 35l, 11l

This time next year we could be salivating over the prospect of a clash between Sprinter Sacre and Simonsig in the Queen Mother Champion Chase.

For now, there are just the inevitable comparisons, some of which were made by trainer Nicky Henderson, who yesterday revealed that this season's novice sensation could head to Cheltenham via the Newbury route successfully trodden last winter by his stablemate.

Just six days on from an exquisite chasing debut at Ascot, Simonsig completed an equally effortless return, making all under Barry Geraghty for a 35-length defeat of the 148-rated Hinterland in the William Hill-backed Wayward Lad Novices' Chase, a contest won 12 months ago by Sprinter Sacre.

From Kempton Sprinter Sacre went to Newbury for the Game Spirit Chase and Simonsig might head the same way after a performance that prompted Boylesports to make him 4-5 favourite from 6-4 for the Racing Post Arkle Chase.

William Hill are evens from 7-4, while Coral are among those offering the best-available 5-4, although the same firm had been happy to quote 2-1 about Sprinter Sacre following his 2011 Christmas win.

'It was a brave shout to run him back so quick, and very un-Henderson-like, but I thought that practice is really all he wants,' said the winning trainer, who had been successful four times at Kempton on Boxing Day.

'That was his first run over two miles but there was never a worry about it. We've always said that when he went over fences it would be over two miles, it's just that over hurdles Barry felt he would be better over two and a half.

'He is doing everything we could ask him to do. He has just won on the bridle. I'm not being rude about the opposition, and Hinterland is not a mug, but we've given him 11lb yet it wasn't a contest.

Simonsig and Barry clear the last at Kempton on just his second start over fences. This was a very polished display only six days after his chasing debut at Ascot.

'Barry said that halfway down the back he thought about me standing in the stands absolutely wetting myself while he was having a lovely time. He summed it up right.'

Asked to sum up Simonsig's standing compared to Sprinter Sacre, Henderson added: 'They have been known to saunter along together but you have to be very careful when you do that. They can help each other but it would be awfully easy for them to do too much.

'They are pretty similar and they both have a lot of speed. Sprinter Sacre went to the Game Spirit before the Arkle and I wouldn't rule it out for this horse. He will definitely have only one more run before Cheltenham, though.'

After that one run will be the Arkle. For Hinterland, perhaps not.

'He was never going to beat Simonsig,' said Paul Nicholls. 'We just wanted to get more experience into him and at least he's now eligible for handicaps. Simonsig is a machine.'

THE ROAD TO CHELTENHAM

Previous spread: Sprinter Sacre causes a splash when returning to the yard with Nico de Boinville after exercise. It was a wet winter and this was only the second time the springs have come up to flood levels. If you look closely at the rug, I haven't changed my name – the initials are stuck on upside down!

IN MID-JANUARY I spoke to the *Post*'s Alastair Down about the importance of Cheltenham to Seven Barrows and my plans for the horses who I hoped would make it a Festival to remember:

If you asked most jumps fans to list Nicky Henderson's seven winners at last year's Festival the headline horses such as Sprinter Sacre, Simonsig and Bobs Worth would trip readily off their tongues but, as the great WA Stephenson never tired of observing, little fish are sweet and the two humblest of his Cheltenham scorers, Une Artiste and Bellvano, carved an important niche in his affections because of the races they won.

Henderson says: 'To win the Fred Winter and the Johnny Henderson Grand Annual was very special to me as they are the two men without whom N Henderson would never have been heard of.

'Dad was very good to me and to racing, most notably in the enormous amount he did for Cheltenham. He absolutely loved his racing and let me go off and try to train racehorses for a living when he knew perfectly well that it was the easiest way in the world to put the family fortunes into meltdown.'

Henderson's mother was killed in the hunting field at the age of 48. He doesn't dwell on it but you can tell that the passing of the years has done little to lessen the freshness of the shock. 'It changed everything,' he recalls, 'and Fred said to me, "You are in a muddle, you better come and work for me."'

Typical Winter that – he was tough as boots but there was a gruff kindness about him that always shone through.

Henderson began training with ten horses – 'most of them mine' – but now the calibre of horse at Seven Barrows is without equal in any yard in the islands. There are seemingly fewer stars in the Milky Way – Bobs Worth, Long Run, Sprinter Sacre, Simonsig and Captain Conan spearhead the chasing strength and there is a three-pronged

Our team of jockeys are invaluable to us at Seven Barrows. At the front are Andrew Tinkler (red jacket) and AP, with Barry (green cap) and David Bass in behind.

Champion Hurdle attack comprising Darlan, Grandouet and Binocular. Throw in a raft of exciting novices and boxloads of live handicap prospects and you have a Festival team of awesome proportions.

For years Henderson has happily fostered the myth that he is not the sharpest on God's earth but brains are not just about intellect and Nicky's mind is the questing type – forever trying to think how he can give his horses the edge and stay ahead of the opposition. As a result there have been changes in the way Long Run has been trained this season and another is afoot.

He says: 'Long Run came through the King George in good form. Nico de Boinville said he felt really well after Kempton whereas it took him a couple of weeks to rediscover his *joie de vivre* following Haydock.

'Nico is both a very good horseman and an excellent schooling jockey and this season we have jumped half a dozen fences a week with Long Run and done a bit less with Yogi Breisner [a jumping expert who helps both horses and jockeys], although we still use Yogi, not least because he is a help to Sam.

'But it has crossed all our minds – Robert Waley-Cohen, Sam and myself – that we should try some headgear with Long Run – cheekpieces I think rather than blinkers. I have been watching him get to the front and then go through a fence, then doss and lose concentration. There is nothing wrong with him being in front and that was the plan at Kempton because we wanted to pre-empt any injection of pace.

'You would school him in cheekpieces just the once and it would be when he does his next piece of work a couple of days later that you would hopefully see the results.'

It says something about the fathom-deep strength at Seven Barrows that Long Run, the Gold Cup winner in 2011 and a dual King George scorer, is the yard's second string behind Bobs Worth, who has won on both his visits to the Festival.

'Bob is amazing because on the racecourse you wouldn't even know he was on the premises then suddenly there he is. If necessary he could go to the Gold Cup without a run as he puts a lot into his races and that takes a lot out of him.'

Having a whole clutch of horses of the highest class in the yard poses its own problems, albeit the sort of problems most trainers would give their eye teeth for. It is the stuff of jumps legend that Tom Dreaper once worked Arkle and Flyingbolt together and that despite their riders' best efforts the two took each other on and frightened the living daylights out of everyone concerned with the result that the exercise was never repeated.

But on the morning I was at Henderson's Darlan had worked with Sprinter Sacre as part of the Champion Chase favourite's build-up to Saturday's Victor Chandler at Ascot and occasionally work mornings are enlivened by a potentially even more explosive pairing.

Henderson says: 'Sprinter Sacre has been all natural talent since the day he got here. When he got beat in his first hurdle he came back with a seriously snotty nose and when he was third in the Supreme I stood in the unsaddling enclosure and said, "Next year this horse will be standing over there where the winner is."

'But Simonsig is a seriously talented horse at home and very occasionally – and only to help them – I have let Sprinter Sacre and Simonsig work together. But you can only do it with work-riders of the quality of Nico and Jerry McGrath.

'Good horses make good horses so to have a bunch at the top end is a help. I have put the two together just a few times and it does frighten you a little bit.

'Within reason good horses help make lesser ones work to a better standard, although obviously it would be pointless pitching some horses in with a Sprinter or a Simonsig. My objective when doing the work list and weights is to do both horses good and there is no point one hammering another ten lengths, you want them finishing together having had a nice time.

'And I can't stress too much the importance of continuity when it comes to work-riders because they get to know their horses so well. Nico rides Long Run and Sprinter and is here full time. Corky loves having him here and when he is breaking horses in it is Nico that he wants to be the first person on their back.

'Simonsig is J McGrath's ride at home and when I was deciding whether to run him at Kempton just six days after he had won his first chase at Ascot I asked him whether the horse was 100 per cent or 99 – and believe me I wouldn't have run if he'd said 99.

'Simonsig is fresh as paint. I'd wanted to leave him alone for a bit but he's been cantering this week as he's so fresh.

'Like other horses of Ronnie Bartlett's he came over from Ian Ferguson in Northern Ireland. Ian does a very good job with them.'

At least part of Henderson's success down the decades has been the presence of two stablemen of enduring repute in the now retired Johnny Worrall and Corky Browne, who has been with Henderson from day one and who the trainer describes as 'legendary'.

Henderson says: 'Corky was at Fred Winter's, he did Killiney and led up Anglo and was very much one of Fred's most trusted men.

'I had been at Fred's five years and was beginning to get itchy feet and one night I went to the pub with Roger Charlton who then owned Windsor House and ran the equine pool there.

'Roger told me that Jeremy Tree wanted him to go to Beckhampton as assistant and said, "Why don't you buy Windsor House and set up on your own?"

'The man running the pool day to day was Corky and Roger said I would be mad not to take him on. Everything that went to the pool was lame to one degree or another and Roger and Corky would mend their legs. Corky has been doing that ever since – I break 'em and he mends 'em.

'He demands high standards and in terms of running the yard he and I are a bit old-fashioned and we do it all in much the same way that Fred would have liked us to. We have evening stables and Corky and I would go round the whole lot together twice a week. He is beyond price.'

Browne is also known to be a major fan of the imposing Captain Conan, who is carded for Sandown's Scilly Isles Novices' Chase over two and a half miles with an eye on the Jewson over the same trip at Cheltenham, leaving Simonsig to do duty in the Racing Post Arkle.

Henderson says: 'Captain Conan is very good. We could hold him up in order to get the trip and I think he would just go to sleep. He works like a very good horse and what's more, he has got gears, although to look at him he'd get three miles in time.'

Time was that the trainer used to get seriously stressed in the run-up to Cheltenham but while he still has his moments he deals with it better than of old. He says: 'It really comes down to how the horses are. If they are flying then it is fine – it's if they are just a little below par that you start to tear your hair out.

'And, of course, we have all been through it before. I still feel young but the fact of the matter is that I am coming to the senior end of this game now. Jumping can be little bit cliquey sometimes but it's actually a big happy family and Cheltenham illustrates that each year with the place full of people from every sort of background and neck of the woods.

'We are in the entertainment business and the object of the exercise is to have fun. The system works here because I have the best owners in the sport and we are all mates. And they are realistic and know that with jumpers things can – and do – go pear-shaped.

'The enthusiasm of the team who own Bobs Worth is literally worth a guinea a minute. They love it and so do I. Long may it last.'

Away from racing and training horses I am involved with the Starlight Foundation, which is a wonderful charity that benefits critically and terminally ill children by granting them a wish. I am joint-chairman, with Christopher Hanbury, of two racedays, one at Newbury in July and the other at Kempton in November. At these racedays we have a big lunch and drum up funds, and we've probably raised in excess of £3 million over the last 20 years. The racing community is incredibly generous when it comes to charities.

The children come up with some wonderful wishes – some are simple to satisfy and some are quite a bit harder – and the charity is very proud that it has never yet turned a wish down or been unable to fulfil it.

It is a great charity to be involved in – but back to the horses, and the story of Bobs Worth is one worth telling. Steve Dennis charted the development of the horse who would become a Cheltenham Gold Cup winner:

Barry, who is pictured here on Bobs Worth, is at Seven Barrows nearly every weekend to get to know the horses. AP, who lives only five miles away, schools all of the horses owned by JP McManus.

If he were human, working in an office somewhere, Bobs Worth would win employee of the month every month, yet half the workforce wouldn't know who he was.

He'd be whispered about at the watercooler, stared at in the canteen, yet he would be oblivious to this and instead would simply go unhurriedly, unworriedly about his work in his habitually efficient, hugely competent and thoroughly unspectacular fashion. His bosses would love him, although the woman at the next desk would find him almost impossible to describe to her friends.

Take, for example, Barry Geraghty. In one way or another Bobs Worth has been part of his life for more than six years, and yet this loquacious and intelligent jockey – an interviewer's delight – flounders like a lovestruck teenager when it comes to putting his finger on the essence of Bobs Worth.

'He's neat, and he does everything neatly,' he says after lengthy consideration, almost shamefacedly, conscious that it isn't a lot to be going on with.

A man in day-to-day contact with the horse finds the task of illustrating life with Bobs Worth just as taxing.

'He's a pleasure to train, although some days you wouldn't know he's there,' he says, to the sound of brains being racked to little avail. 'He's very straightforward, no issues or quirks – he's just a very nice person.'

So in this era of hysterical media attention and forensic examination of personality, who is this neat, nice person who is favourite for the Betfred Cheltenham Gold Cup? We knew Kauto Star and Denman almost intimately, had daily updates on Frankel, but Bobs Worth stays resolutely under the radar despite his already considerable achievements.

The eight-year-old came to us not by the predictable routes of a French hurdle or an Irish point-to-point, but in the more traditional sphere of the 'store horse'. Geraghty, working with his brother Norman, was in the market for two or three yearlings at Tattersalls in November 2006 and picked up the bay son of Bob Back for €16,500.

'He didn't stick out a mile,' recalls Geraghty, not unexpectedly. 'He wasn't very big, but he was a very correct and active walker, he had a good way of going.

'He had a nice pedigree – that's the thing that would attract you more than anything, by Bob Back from an old Jim Bolger pedigree. We were trying to buy something we could make a profit on and I thought he was good value.'

Bobs Worth spent the next two and a half years turned out at Geraghty's home near Fairyhouse, just a young store growing up slowly. Geraghty never sat on him, never trotted him over a line of poles. He took him to Goffs sales in June 2008 but brought him home again, then sent him to Doncaster in May 2009 as a four-year-old hurdling prospect.

'He was always a really nice sort growing up, although not physically imposing,' says Geraghty. 'I mentioned him to Nicky when he was a three-year-old and he'd already caught Nicky's eye before I got to Doncaster. I didn't have to twist his arm to buy him.

'We probably bought him at the top of the market. When we went to sell him at Goffs the market was slipping away. Look, we were happy enough to cover the cost price, I saw a lot of people lose money on their deals at around that time. We washed our face with him and that was fine by us.'

For the remarkably reasonable price of £20,000, Bobs Worth left Geraghty and joined Henderson. Now he needed an owner – enter the five-strong Not Afraid Partnership, comprising Malcolm Kimmins, Caro Wells, John Jarvis, David Nash and Nick Deacon, for whom it was a first venture into ownership. The Not Afraiders do know fear, Kimmins points out, it's just that they used to own the useful hurdler Afrad and the name of the syndicate indicated the response to the inevitable question.

'We were looking for another horse,' says Kimmins, 76, who says he's 'nominally in charge' of the partnership and has been since the death of Nigel Clark – 'to whom we owe a million thanks' – five years ago.

'Nicky bought three at Doncaster and we looked at all three, but Caro was particularly sweet on Bobs Worth and she pushed us towards him. So we had him – we could easily have taken one of the other two. It was an extraordinary bit of luck.'

Kimmins adopts the customary stance towards Bobs Worth – 'Initially, no-one was particularly excited about him,' he admits – whose name came to him like an alarm in the middle of the night. Perhaps we should point out to younger readers that a 'bob' is slang for the pre-decimal shilling, 12 old pence, a handy piece of silver but no-one's idea of a fortune. If Kimmins and co had been hoping for a return in keeping with their horse's name, the reality would turn out to be a wonderful surprise.

Geraghty was looking forward to renewing acquaintance both on the Seven Barrows gallops and on his debut at Kempton in February 2010. As for any debutant, the education is more important than the result, and Bobs Worth – third favourite for a bumper behind stablemate Prince Of Pirates and a certain Captain Chris – was there primarily for a nice day out.

'Prince Of Pirates had been burning up the gallops, he was all the talk and no-one had been singing about Bobs Worth,' says Geraghty.

'But he gave the favourite a little bit to think about and was beaten only a length and a half. It was very encouraging and I got a good kick out of him running well.'

Kimbo – Malcolm Kimmins, part-owner of Bobs Worth – feeling no pain at the press conference the morning after the Cheltenham Gold Cup, having watched the video of the race 52 times during the night!

Bobs Worth returned to Kempton two months later to win a bumper, and went back there for a third time for his hurdling debut the following November, which is when a little seed of hope began to take root among the Not Afraiders. He won there, won twice at Cheltenham – beating future Champion Hurdle winner Rock On Ruby on the second occasion – before taking his place in the Albert Bartlett Novices' Hurdle at the Festival. He won that too, although given the heights to which he has since climbed the Albert Bartlett has been relatively overshadowed.

His progress through the ranks of novice chasers was less implacable, although through no fault of his own, and Henderson recalled the situation in an interview in the *Racing Post Annual.*

'He had a wind operation after finishing third in the Feltham – Barry wasn't happy with his breathing – and it knocked him sideways.

'He looked dreadful. In mid-January I thought he had no chance whatsoever of getting to Cheltenham, we just had to leave him alone and hope he'd find a way back.

'In the end I had to get a run into him and he ran well in the Reynoldstown, but then the question was how well he'd come back from that. He just got there – his coat was right for the first time in months on the Wednesday morning.'

Bobs Worth is the first horse since Flyingbolt in the 1960s to win at three consecutive Cheltenham Festivals in different races. Above he is pictured on the way to winning the Albert Bartlett Novices' Hurdle in 2011 and below after winning the RSA Chase in 2012. After winning the Gold Cup in 2013 he is now unbeaten in five starts at Cheltenham.

On the Wednesday afternoon Bobs Worth won the
RSA Chase by a quietly accomplished two and a half lengths.
The words 'quietly accomplished' sum the horse up; without
remotely waxing lyrical, because this horse embodies the
suffragette dictum, 'Deeds not words'.

Geraghty sheds light on his ultra-efficient, ultra-consistent
partner. 'It's difficult to sing about him but he feels like a
good horse when I'm sitting on him. He just does all that
he has to do – if you want him to go quicker he'll go quicker,
if you don't he'll stay the same pace,' he says, the words
coming more easily now.

'He never gives the impression he's about to take the field
apart, but that's what he ends up doing. He has a little bit of
everything, he jumps and travels nicely, he stays well – put
something in front of him and he'll beat it.

'I'm probably better riding him a little bit conservatively.
He might let you believe he's slow but he has more pace than
you think, and that enables me to ride him quite confidently.

'He's not the scopiest individual, I'd never be looking for
big Sprinter Sacre-like leaps, but he's very, very good from
A to B and, when I need him to, he can go A to C.'

At Newbury on Hennessy day he ran the whole gamut
as far as Kimmins is concerned. There may be two Cheltenham
Festival wins on Bobs Worth's roll of honour but the Hennessy
is the high point for local boy Kimmins.

'To me it's the most exciting race in the calendar,' he says.
'It's the race to win – give me the Hennessy over the Grand
National any time, it's such a fair race, such a great race.

'I must confess I watch the recording of the Hennessy
most days. It made it extra special to have Bobs Worth's
breeder there too – Lois Eadie is based in County Fermanagh
and has had such joy and pleasure from the horse's successes.
Her husband Roland was at Newbury too and we have all
had huge fun together.

'Barry, who rides him so beautifully, said, "This horse
is what racing's all about," and I loved that comment. I also
enjoyed hearing Nick Luck on Racing UK say, "This horse
just does not get beaten."'

Bobs Worth is relatively lightly raced for an eight-year-
old – the Hennessy was only his 11th race – and Henderson

points out his uncomplicated work ethic means he never gives himself an easy time of it.

'He gives you more than most horses, he puts a lot into his races and it's hard work for him,' he says. 'He's not the biggest, not the most robust of horses. It just means we have to be a bit mindful of where we go with him, we have to be careful how he takes his races.

'He wouldn't do a huge amount of work at home although he's very professional in what he does do. He just gets on with it without being flashy or spectacular.

'If all you could judge him on was what he does at home you'd never know he was such a good horse. He doesn't show it here – he's no Simonsig or Oscar Whisky on the gallops – he saves it for the racecourse.'

It's a thoroughly unsurprising character assessment, serving merely to reinforce the notion that here is a true game-day player, no morning glory but an afternoon delight. Yet, given Bobs Worth's comparative inexperience, Geraghty is still learning about him, and what he gleaned at Newbury provides encouragement when the conversation turns, as it must, to the Gold Cup.

'The Hennessy was his first run in a big, competitive field over fences,' he says. 'I've always kept him wide in his races because he's not a big, imposing sort and I didn't want to stick him in a pocket, but at some stage you have to take the bull by the horns and take your chance down the inner.

'He fought his corner at Newbury, showed plenty of courage, and he'll have to do that in the Gold Cup – and, without wanting to get too soppy about it, of course it gives me massive satisfaction to know that I bought the Gold Cup favourite as a yearling.'

The Not Afraid Partnership – who also have novice hurdler Chatterbox in their Festival portfolio – are scanning the future too, and despite Kimmins describing himself as a pessimist he can't keep the hope out of his voice.

'It's incredible to have the Gold Cup favourite. I have to pinch myself almost daily,' he says. 'He's not a brilliant price mind, although I'm not a punter. But how many horses will come up the hill as he can? I've owned horses for 50 years, started off with Fulke Walwyn, and I thought I'd seen it all happen. In this instance, though, it's happened to us.

'I'll lose sleep, I'm well known for being a boxwalker. God knows how I'll get through the day and I wish the race was on the Tuesday and not the Friday.

'I'll have to watch it through my fingers. If you have lots of horses I dare say you might get used to it – but I really can't see how anyone could get used to it.'

Naturally, Geraghty is used to it, but at the moment his biggest concern is finding the right words to describe Bobs Worth, this seemingly ordinary yet quite extraordinary horse. He plays with the faint-praise likes of 'efficient', 'unassuming', 'a thrill to ride' and 'competent' before the light of certainty comes on in his eyes.

There's no doubt it's the right phrase, that he's got Bobs Worth to a tee, that this is all you need to know. 'He never lets you down,' says Geraghty, and he's right.

One funny story from Bobs Worth's bumper debut is what JP Magnier, who rode the favourite Prince Of Pirates, said afterwards. As Barry has recalled, Prince Of Pirates was deserved favourite and Bobs was any price you liked. I told JP to follow Barry on Bobs Worth as he knew where the best ground would be and then between the wings of what would have been the last two flights to join Barry and let Prince Of Pirates go.

Roles somehow reversed early on with Barry tracking JP and cruising up to him two out. I was thinking 'Oh my God, everyone has backed Prince Of Pirates'. With about 100 yards to go Barry was still there when JP finally gives his horse a couple of nudges and he won by a length and a half. I asked JP what happened and he said: 'I didn't want to take my hands off because I didn't want to fall off.' He is a great guy and loved his riding until a fall ended his career in the saddle.

We were thrilled with Bobs Worth's Hennessy win, but he had a slightly dull period after that, which was no problem, and he was certainly far better than he was the previous season when he simply fell to pieces. He wasn't on the radar at all.

He probably doesn't have the strongest constitution, but this season he had a much clearer run through to

Cheltenham, although he did miss Trials Day because of a bad scope. At the time the weather didn't help many of our horses because it was so bad and even if racing was on it was often too soft to run them.

We were snowed in before Christmas, but we were able to exercise the horses indoors and when the snow was on the ground that's what we did.

Lambourn was severely tested as the heavy snow continued into January and Rodney Masters reported on how everyone, not just myself, was coping with the adverse conditions:

Snowdrifts were measured at five to six feet. You could walk along the hedgerow tops. A helicopter dropped off supplies of bread and milk. But that was Lambourn on January 18, exactly 50 years ago. The last of the snow at the training centre did not thaw until the week after the 2,000 Guineas in May.

By comparison, yesterday's near 13cm (five inches) was little more than a chilly irritation for racing's workforce. Indeed, for many villagers snowfall came as a welcome diversion from the more testing weather-related problem that has cursed the valley since soon after Christmas.

Chalk springs erupted with more ferocity than at any time in the past 30 years. They popped up in the most unexpected places. Much to his surprise, one suddenly sprang to life under the carpet in the living room at Jamie Osborne's home in Upper Lambourn.

At a time when the Environment Agency was downgrading most of its flood warnings in Britain, one river appeared in the opposite column, the River Lambourn.

However, neither flooded lanes nor yesterday's snowfall has caused more than a hiccup to the training schedule. Most yards sent out at least a couple of lots yesterday, thanks to the exhaustive around-the-clock endeavour of Will Riggall and his team at Jockey Club Estates, who kept the all-weather gallops operational.

Hungerford Hill, the main route to the M4, was closed by police after a tractor and trailer jackknifed, but with a little determination most other roads remained passable. No helicopter was needed by Ocado driver David

HENDERSON'S HEROES

Oliver, who made it to all his online grocery customers in the valley. 'If one route is blocked you find another,' he said cheerily.

How was it yesterday for a young member of racing's workforce experiencing her first winter in Lambourn? Emily Melbourn, 20, from Nottingham, joined Mark Usher in August to progress her career as an apprentice jockey. 'I thought it was cold at minus three the other day, but Jodie Hayward, who is one of our senior work-riders, was telling me it dropped to minus 13 a couple of winters back.

'It didn't feel too cold today and the snow was all right because it arrived quite late on. The secret of coping with the cold is lots of layers of clothing with a lycra base. I have a ride at Kempton tomorrow. I'm praying it's on.'

That wicked winter of 1963 is etched indelibly in the memory of Corky Browne. 'I was 20 at the time and it was my first winter in Britain. I was living in a caravan at Fred Winter's and if I could have got out of Lambourn I'd never have come back. But that was it, there was no escape because all roads were blocked. There was no M4. Helicopters dropped food to us.'

Another with a vivid memory of that never-ending winter is George 'Darkie' Deacon, 83, who was Fulke Walwyn's head man. 'Because the weather didn't relent until March many people reckoned horses trained in Ireland would clean up at Cheltenham.

'But we sent five horses to the meeting and had three winners, including Mill House in the Gold Cup, and two seconds. In the worst of the weather we'd oiled the horses' feet and exercise them on the harrowed snow.'

Nicky Henderson may well take note of Deacon's encouraging Festival statistic should these conditions persist. Meanwhile, Browne said yesterday the Seven Barrows horses would probably canter on the snow this morning.

The weather relented enough for Cheltenham to stage Trials Day at the end of January, where Sprinter Sacre delivered another faultless performance in the rescheduled Victor Chandler Chase. Graham Dench reported for the *Post*:

Overleaf: Brrrrr! I look on as Nico walks Sprinter Sacre around the covered ring in driving snow. It shows how useful the covered ride can be when the weather is as bad as it was in the winter of 2012–13.

Victor Chandler Chase
2m ½f

1 Sprinter Sacre   1-5f
Barry Geraghty

2 Mad Moose   50-1
Sam Twiston-Davies

3 Somersby   8-1
Dominic Elsworth

Distances 14l, 2¼l

Nicky Henderson was so nervous before the Victor Chandler Chase he said he would have paid £1 million to take Sprinter Sacre home.

He need not have been. Chasing win number seven, in a race postponed from the previous Saturday and switched from Ascot, proved as effortless as all the others. Indeed, odds of 1-4 were soon looking generous as, having jumped past Mad Moose at the first open ditch down the far side, Sprinter Sacre was barely out of second gear as he bowled along in a clear lead, with Somersby, Sanctuaire and the four others in a depleted field all toiling.

It was another flawless performance from the seven-year-old, who now heads straight to the Sportingbet Queen Mother Champion Chase, a race jockey Barry Geraghty has won four times already, including twice on Moscow Flyer.

Coral and BetVictor make him a 1-4 chance for an eighth straight win there and the 2-5 from Boylesports, Paddy Power and William Hill looks almost a case of buying money, if there is such a thing ante-post.

As Sprinter Sacre returned to a reception of Festival proportions, having beaten the rallying Mad Moose as he pleased by 14 lengths, Henderson admitted: 'I'm glad it's over. I didn't have any reservations about running but Barry was worried about the ground and I was worried he was a bit fresh.

'I didn't expect Sanctuaire to go on this time and I didn't really want to make it. But with this horse you can't do anything but use his jumping and his galloping.

'I said to Barry if he takes you there just let him go. We're all bricking it in the stands, but Barry says it's absolutely wonderful, the best fun in the world…

'We needed this and it's important to say well done to Cheltenham, to Ascot and to Victor Chandler. We needed this staged, but you can't do it without everyone rowing the boat together. I can switch the engine off the aeroplane for a week now.'

Geraghty described Sprinter Sacre's win as 'brilliant' and added: 'I was very hopeful the ground wouldn't be an issue, although it was in the back of my mind. But he travelled and jumped so easily and was so relaxed.

Sprinter Sacre (above) at his magisterial best in the Victor Chandler Chase at Cheltenham, January 2013. The snow is still on Cleeve Hill, but at least we are racing. In the winner's enclosure afterwards (right) owner Caroline Mould is pictured between Barry and myself.

'When I got on him before the race I was trying not to get too excited, but he's so gorgeous, even the way he walks. "Moscow" was brilliant, but I'd say he's nearly level pegging.'

Looking ahead, Henderson said: 'Cheltenham will be only his third race [of the season], but Aintree is two and a half miles, so Punchestown will possibly come into the equation. You can see why he's not a two-and-a-half mile horse. He's pure speed, it would be like asking Frankel to go a mile and a half. Why do it?'

The JP McManus-owned Darlan was made second favourite for the Champion Hurdle after his win at Kempton and we chose a race at Doncaster at the beginning of February for his Cheltenham prep. However, he made a fatal last-hurdle mistake and his death was, by miles, the lowest point of the whole season. He was seriously good, he could have been very special indeed and I think he'd have won the Champion Hurdle. He was a beautiful, gorgeous-looking horse who had everything. I don't think I've ever seen AP hit as hard as that.

At the races Minty said, 'You'd better come and have a drink', but it was February, when I always stop drinking for a month, so I just got into the car and went home. I got about a thousand text messages of sympathy and they were all gratefully received, but as usual it was simply a case of having to get up the next morning and get on with it.

Looking back now, the atmosphere in the yard in the days afterwards was subdued to say the least. But the support we had from throughout the racing world was overwhelming. That certainly helped us to pick up and press on. Sadly, Darlan was without doubt one of the brightest lights we've ever had here.

We all know the risks involved, but nothing in the world can take away the pain of an empty box. That applies to any horse that doesn't come home, but when it is one as good as Darlan it's not surprisingly that much harder to bear. Our team were devastated, especially Andy Llewellyn who looked after Darlan and rode him every day. I know how devastated AP was, as of course was JP, who I spoke to in America the day it happened and who cares about his horses more than anybody I know.

Legendary owner JP McManus, who numbered the ill-fated Darlan and My Tent Or Yours among so many other top-class horses I've been lucky enough to train for him. Here he is in the winner's enclosure after Binocular's 2010 Champion Hurdle with his wife Noreen, AP and lad Robin Land.

JP and I had spent the previous summer discussing whether to go chasing or to see if he was a horse for the Champion Hurdle. Obviously we took the latter route rather than the novice chase one. I've no doubt he would have become a very bright star as a chaser.

Darlan simply didn't have a fault in him. You couldn't have asked for a nicer horse with a nicer temperament. We all miss him enormously.

The irony of it all was that we lost a star on the Monday and on Saturday a new star was born when My Tent Or Yours won the Betfair Hurdle at Newbury for JP and AP. Rodney Masters reported:

Tony McCoy ended a horrific week on a high, and even with a flicker of a smile, when My Tent Or Yours showed such stunning power in the Betfair Hurdle that he was introduced at a price as short as 6-1 for the Stan James Champion Hurdle – for which he would require a supplementary entry.

After a performance in which he could be called the winner three flights out, many punters will assume that the novice will fill the void at Cheltenham left by Monday's casualty Darlan, but McCoy, in the immediate debrief, sounded as if he would suggest to owner JP McManus that it may be prudent to wait until next season.

Betfair Hurdle (Handicap)
2m ½f

1 My Tent Or Yours   5-1f
AP McCoy

2 Cotton Mill   9-1
Jack Quinlan (3)

3 Swing Bowler   8-1
Timmy Murphy

4 Dark Lover   16-1
Ryan Mahon (3)

Distances 5l, 1¼l, 2¼l

My Tent Or Yours is 7-4 with the sponsor for the William Hill Supreme Novices' Hurdle, usurping the same owner's recent recruit Jezki, who was pushed out to 9-2 by Hills.

'I'd be quite happy to win the Supreme this year and wait until next season for the Champion,' said McCoy. 'This is a very good horse and it was a great run for a novice off that rating, but this is a handicap and there's still a way to go.'

McCoy, whose mount slammed Cotton Mill and co by five lengths and up, said he had spent a morning educating My Tent Or Yours at trainer Nicky Henderson's Seven Barrows base to prepare for this challenge.

'About ten days ago I schooled him in behind a group of horses to get him ready for competing in a big field,' McCoy revealed. 'He did learn a lot that day and it helped here.

'If the ground had been good I'd have been confident, but in this ground I was worried about getting home because he can take a very strong hold.'

Asked about the loss of Darlan, he added: 'It has been a horrific week for everyone. It's the most difficult part of the sport to cope with. But you have to get on with it.'

Corky Browne, making a rare visit to the races, agreed with McCoy that there was no need to rush their winner into the Champion, saying: 'I'd like to see him go for the Supreme – one step at a time.'

It was a record fifth Betfair Hurdle win for Henderson, who said: 'This horse can be terribly keen but he has got gears and can quicken up. I'm sure the better the ground the better he'll be.

'We hadn't thought about the Champion Hurdle. It has been a difficult week losing Darlan. I know how much that hurt JP and AP, and everyone back at home. It will be a boost for us all to have another horse with the potential to go to the top.'

The trainer added: 'Go back a year and Darlan looked like winning this race for the same team until falling two out. We'd all hoped Darlan was a horse for the Champion Hurdle, and hopefully this is one for the race next year.'

One of the many things we're blessed with at Seven
Barrows is a wonderful set of jockeys. There's Barry,
of course, Andrew Tinkler, who's never ridden better,
and David Bass, who is something of a demon drummer
on his nights off.

Nico de Boinville rides work on Sprinter Sacre and
Long Run and ended up champion amateur. But he had
been getting frustrated until one ride on Petit Robin in a
televised Saturday race at Sandown Park in December gave
him a huge boost and changed his whole career. We also

have Richie Killoran, Jerry McGrath and Freddie Mitchell – my owners never put pressure on me to go outside the yard, they're loyal to my jockeys and loyal to the core, and that is so important. It makes everything so much simpler.

Unfortunately, sometimes you can't hang on to them all, all the way through – they want to move on and get a leg-up somewhere else because that's only human nature, but at the moment I couldn't be happier with my lot. I've got the best bunch of horses I've ever had and the best bunch of jockeys too.

In the middle of February Brough Scott visited Seven Barrows to find out more about Nico de Boinville:

Why risk the guaranteed glories of the morning for the uncertain promises of the afternoon? No young rider has faced this dilemma more exactly than amateur jockey Nico de Boinville, who is aboard Long Run and Sprinter Sacre every day after sunrise but who will pitch himself into the professional jockeys' arena after Cheltenham.

At the moment the 23-year-old from Hampshire starts his morning with the most envied and most important dual role racing can offer as Festival fever rages to its March conclusion. Long Run and Sprinter Sacre are the greatest of all the stars that sparkle in the Nicky Henderson string. Both are already champions in their category.

Long Run is out to regain the Gold Cup he won in 2011 and Sprinter Sacre is ready to extend his unbeaten record over fences by winning the Queen Mother Champion Chase. But both are also big, powerful steeplechasers drawing almost 550 kilos on the weighbridge and neither are the sort you would want to mess about.

'They are both quite straightforward to ride,' says de Boinville, 'but they both like their own space indoors. I think a lot of good horses can be like that. Long Run can be quite moody and grumpy in his box and Sprinter is always threatening to kick the crap out of Sarwah Mohammed who does him.

'They are both magnificent, big horses but they are different shapes to ride. Long Run does not have so much in front of you, but there is so much power behind that he would actually

Nico de Boinville: the work-rider of Long Run and Sprinter Sacre who had a very successful season and finished champion amateur – then turned professional for the 2013–14 season.

be a little heavier than Sprinter Sacre, who has this tremendous neck and shoulder but is not quite as solid beneath.

'They are different in their work too,' he says with the informed voice of the boxing second rather than a mere admiring bottle-carrier. 'Long Run can pull hard for a furlong but after that he will only do as much as you ask him.

'Sprinter Sacre takes a good solid jumper's pull and you have to be sure to keep the handbrake on so that he does not do too much. It is a fantastic privilege to be riding horses like these,' he adds. 'I only took on Long Run last year after Tom Symonds left to go training on his own. Long Run was very much Tom's baby but I have been with Sprinter Sacre ever since he was a raw bumper horse who had come over as part of a job lot from France.

'I was the first to school him over fences and while Long Run is brilliant and I won't have those who slate his jumping, Sprinter is out of this world. I have never, will never, sit on anything like him.'

For many people this dual responsibility would be dreams enough but the young man who occupies the most important saddles of a morning rages with other thoughts about the afternoons. 'I know I am quite unhealthily ambitious,' he says of his plan to abandon his attractive amateur status, which last week led to him being invited up north to ride at Musselburgh and Kelso, 'but I can't continue as I am and I'm determined to give it my all.'

They are good words but there is a sad familiarity about them as they echo so many young butterflies that are soon broken on jump racing's brutal wheel. Just as only one in a thousand of the four-legged symbols of promise ever make it to any sort of eminence on the track, so only very few of the would-be champions of the saddle make it to the higher plateaus of the game as fortune and injuries batter the body and torment the soul. But de Boinville has a back-story every bit as intriguing as the two champions he rides out over the Lambourn Downs. For a start he too has a serious French connection.

Indeed, it goes back a fair bit further than either the story of Long Run's dam Libertina, who bred Sam Waley-Cohen's life-changing Mildmay of Flete winner Liberthine, or Sprinter Sacre's mother Fatima III, who was the only mare owned by her breeder Christophe Masle. The Chastel de Boinvilles go back to the guillotine. If it hadn't been for the French Revolution, it might be Nicolai rather than the Holy Sisters of the Convent who now reside in the family chateau in the Lorraine. Quite a few heads did roll into the guillotine's basket but the de Boinvilles who got to London were made of pretty special stuff and, although he is anxious only to be judged as a potential jockey, there appears to be plenty of that ingredient in the rider who bears their name.

He may be a privately educated son of privilege but he has been little short of a prodigy both in the saddle and the schoolroom. His father works in the City, his mother runs the local Montessori School attended by Andrew Balding's children, and exams are clearly not a problem. De Boinville won an Open Scholarship to Bradfield and top marks in three A-levels meant he sailed up to Newcastle as a high achiever. But his absolute favourite subject was not on the curriculum. As an actor he had played all sorts of lead roles in school productions, yet the part of the free-wheeling student proved to be beyond him.

'He didn't just like riding, he needed it,' says his mother Shaunagh with a mixture of wonder and concern. 'Of course it was in the genes a bit, my sister Philippa rode at Badminton and I was on the British dressage squad. But Nico was completely obsessed with it.

'He was rising at the trot before he was two. He would have been hyperactive if it hadn't been for ponies. When he was nine years old he was supreme champion in the Search for a Star class at the Horse of the Year show at Wembley on a six-year-old first pony who had not been off the leading rein six months earlier. When he was about ten he came in and said, "I have ridden five ponies this morning but I wish it had been seven and all at Wembley."'

Shaunagh's efforts to steer her children into the less risky world of dressage were rewarded by de Boinville winning the junior section and being third overall in the Pony Club Dressage Championships. But her sister's example was soon followed by her son competing eagerly in events and team chases and, worse still, the fact that Philippa's husband was the trainer Patrick Chamings and that Nico's grandfather was an ardent watcher of racing on television meant that Mrs de Boinville was unlikely to dowse the siren call of the racing game. For his gap year, the would-be politics graduate went to work with trainer Richard Gibson in Chantilly. It was not the sort of epiphany a schoolteacher would plan, but it was a life-changer all right.

'He worked the butt off me,' says de Boinville, whose lean cheeks have a red blush about them as if the student face was still surprised by so much open air.

'But I woke up every morning looking at the chateau, he took me everywhere, I rode a lot and I had to really learn French. What's more Richard gave me two rides at Fontainebleau who finished second and third, although I did smack my nose coming out of the stalls on the first one and finished with blood all over my silks.'

Bloodied in every sense, de Boinville came back across the Channel with a new focus that conjured a couple of rides for Chamings and two for near neighbour Andrew Balding, one of whom, Western Roots at Newbury on August 3, 2008, etched himself forever in the mind as the first winner of the jockey's career.

Nico is led in on Petit Robin after winning the 2m Listed hurdle at Sandown Park in December 2012. Petit Robin was part-owned by Ken Knox, who had supported Nico in his early years when he gave him rides in point-to-points.

Following the story so far it might seem an obvious, almost easy leap to the present position where Mr N de Boinville is the most sought after amateur in Britain, has ridden headline winners for his mentor Nicky Henderson, and whose televised success at Ffos Las on Carruthers two weeks ago took his prize-money total to more than £100,000.

In fact, the four and a half years in between have been racked by so much perceived failure and frustration that in November he told Henderson he was intent on returning to France unless things turned out better than the two winners and just 15 rides he had managed to glean from the famous Seven Barrows stable since he joined in 2009.

'I said I thought that he was being a bit hasty,' says the trainer in that jocular manner that doesn't quite conceal a profound knowledge of the business. 'Of course he was getting frustrated but I had always told him that there could be no promises. And anyway he then got on Petit Robin in a big handicap at Sandown in December and he kept the ride on him to be second in the Ladbroke at Ascot and fifth in the Betfair last week at Newbury.

'From the very beginning you could see he was a natural horseman. Corky was on to him straight away to get started with our babies. He had lovely hands but what was missing was racing experience. Being a good rider is one thing, being a race-rider is another.

'Now he looks as if he has given himself a chance.'

In fact, the frustration had been building since long before the Seven Barrows showdown and had begun with a real crisis not three months after that thrilling first victory at Newbury. De Boinville went up to Newcastle and hated every minute of it. After six weeks he came home and told his parents he could not go on. 'He was in a very bad place both physically and mentally,' says his mother, 'and it took him some time to get together again. But we had a point-to-pointer he got started on and he spent a lot of time with my brother-in-law. Then in the summer of 2009 he approached Nicky Henderson.'

The trainer was frank. He said de Boinville could come and work but there could be no guarantee of race-rides. In fact there was just one that first season, five more the next, and just nine last term – albeit with the high-profile benefit of two victories on the Queen's horse Barbers Shop. This season there have been only seven more rides for the stable but the successes on Petit Robin and State Benefit have been the very best of calling cards.

'When I first met the guv'nor,' says de Boinville, 'he said he already had six jockeys but he did leave me with one phrase – "Remember the cream always rises to the top." It's been very frustrating with absolutely no winners. But in 2011 I was lucky enough to be picked for Britain in the international Fegentri championship, travelled a lot and rode a winner in Norway. At the beginning of this season the guv'nor got me linked up with agent Dave Roberts, who has been a big help in getting me outside rides. I claim 7lb and said I would ride anything so I was doing 9st 7lb and scrubbing round the back but I was at last getting some practice.'

The arrival of Roberts on the scene has brought a tighter focus to de Boinville's career in more ways than one. This month a bill for £700 arrived for the agent's share of the money won by the jockey's horses but which, being an amateur, the rider cannot receive.

Turning professional may be full of risk but at this juncture it is the only affordable option, and with possibilities in the offing there is the chance that he can get the kick-start of promotion that only a Festival winner can give.

All credit to him for trying. Racing never has much space for faint hearts and it will be truly fascinating to see if de Boinville can fashion himself fresh opportunities out of the profile his current position still gives and add a winning edge to the easy flowing, rounded horsemanship that is already his trademark. 'I like his attitude when we are schooling together,' says Barry Geraghty. 'He is always riding for the horse, not to try to attract attention to himself. He lets the fences come to him and gets the horse to learn to pop. If someone had got excited and put a gun to Sprinter Sacre's head he could have been a long time learning. Nico was the man who started him.'

Henderson can't promise anything and neither should he. But what he does do is give the very best of references. 'He is a very committed and serious young man,' he says of de Boinville, 'and the part he and the other good riders play in the training process cannot be overestimated. You like to leave the same people on these good horses because they know the small things. There may be only the tiniest of things wrong, so tiny that another rider would not even notice. But it's spotting these tiny things that can make all the difference.'

Nico de Boinville is about to embark on one of the most unforgiving challenges in sport. He brings great gifts with him but they will not stop the falls and fractures and falsehoods that lie between him and the glorious uplands where the champions reign.

The odds, as always, are against him. But the best way to shorten them is to first make his present role a winning one. 'To be riding horses like Long Run and Sprinter Sacre every morning means that they are always in the forefront of your mind – and they are just two. Compared to all those that the guv'nor must have going round his head, I have an easy job.'

We were edging closer to Cheltenham and I did seven preview nights in nine days, I think, and there was one spectacular one we did in Glasgow, organised by Ronnie

Bobs Worth (Barry), Long Run (Nico) and Binocular (AP) work over two miles at Kempton in February. Clerk of the course Barney Clifford was kind enough to let us work after racing on the grass. We needed to do this because of the interrupted preparation we had suffered in the spring.

Bartlett. It was a glittering cast-list – Nick Luck, AP, me, Barry, Charlie Swan, Arthur Moore – and the place was full of 700 Glaswegians.

They were a great crowd – luckily it was February so I was off the booze – and at one point this guy got up to ask me a question and I have to say I didn't understand one single, solitary word. It was delivered in the broadest Glaswegian and he was hopelessly pissed. Everyone just creased up laughing. It was a hysterical night.

What they all want is a tip, so what I do is give a different tip at each preview night and hopefully at least one lot of people will be happy. I said my banker was 'Ruby to be leading jockey'…Barry said, 'Thanks a lot, boss.' I got that one right, though!

As well as attending preview nights, we always do a press day at Seven Barrows to run through my plans for the media. Tom Kerr was present for the *Post:*

Intense media interest and appearances at Festival preview evenings are all part of the build-up to Cheltenham. Clare Balding and Mick visited Seven Barrows for Channel 4 Racing – and it's great to see Mick thriving in his new media career. To us he still feels part of the place.

The great chestnut tree that stands in the middle of the main quadrangle at Nicky Henderson's Sevens Barrows has seen many winters come and go, but seldom have its barren branches gazed down on such a show of talent as paraded before the media yesterday.

There is Long Run, the resurgent 2011 Gold Cup winner who has amassed an army of followers almost as large as the horde of doubters arrayed against him. He may be a flawed talent, but he is also a champion, and you sense few things would give greater pleasure than making him so again.

His exhaustive preparation consists of more than just trips up and down the gallop. He and Binocular, the 2010 Champion Hurdle winner, were recently stuck in a horsebox by Henderson and driven 'twice around the village'.

'They didn't know where they were but they were only the other side of the hedge,' Henderson says. They'll know where they are next month, you'd expect.

Binocular comes out to pose with Grandouet, his Champion Hurdle rival, and the two begin to square up to each other like a pair of prize-fighters. 'Hello, have you met?' says Henderson as he separates the pair, half-trainer, half-bouncer. 'They don't seem to like each other. Have your argument halfway up the hill.'

The parade, put on primarily for the almost dozen television camera crews that have converged on Lambourn, is old hat for the staff at Seven Barrows, who launch a concerted campaign to attract the horses' attention.

One pads about in the background shaking a wooden horse with bells on it and a sign reading 'Long Run' (Gold Cup favourite he may not be, but he's still boss here), while Sophie theatrically opens and closes an umbrella. Despite their best efforts some horses are reluctant to play the game, earning a sharp rebuke of 'Pay attention!' from their trainer, who plays the game very well.

Understandably, it is Sprinter Sacre who gets the biggest showing, pictured alone with Henderson for several minutes, the pair trying out different poses like young lovers playing around in a photo booth.

'He's just a gorgeous horse with a lot of natural talent,' coos Henderson. 'It's all very easy for him. He loves doing it.'

Then there is World Hurdle joint-favourite Oscar Whisky, who would probably prefer a race half a mile shorter.

Henderson is 'still campaigning for a Ryanair Hurdle', but in the meantime Oscar Whisky must make do.

Bobs Worth is 'on schedule' for the Gold Cup but will probably have to improve again to win a 'very open' race.

Simonsig, alone of all of them, is fed a handful of delicious carrots (a clue?). My Tent Or Yours looks a picture, but talk soon turns to Darlan. Poor My Tent Or Yours, he is like the twin that lived; he must achieve for two and could just do it. It is some force. As Henderson says: 'I've got an army and they're all ready to go.' But is it enough to hope to repeat last year's extraordinary seven Festival winners?

*Previous spread: working
Sprinter Sacre and Simonsig
together can be quite a
dangerous thing to do as it
would be easy for them to
race one another. Here they
are working over a mile on
the Faringdon Road gallop
and finishing together on
the bridle.*

'Completely and utterly impossible,' says Henderson.
'You would settle for one and don't dare dream for more.
The best thing to do is find one on the first day and the
confidence grows. I don't know why that could make
them run faster.' And the worst case scenario: 'You'd
be suicidal on a blank.'

Henderson is a ball of nerves and excitement at this time
of year, which is perhaps the reason Sophie says that while he
trains the horses, she 'tries to train the trainer'. Is that more
difficult than training the horses? 'It can be.'

She adds: 'It is all consuming but actually he loves it, just
loves it. Of course everyone gets anxious and it's the pressure
of having such magnificent horses. That's the thing that amazes
me, the enthusiasm.'

The excitement infects the entire team at Seven Barrows,
including Henderson's driver Neil 'The Wheel' Taylor, who
of necessity spends many hours ferrying his boss around the
country. 'Everyone's on edge a little bit, hoping they all stay
in one piece. They're such fragile animals,' he says, meaning
the horses, not his passenger.

Who does Taylor hope to see triumph next month?
'Grandouet is a bit of a favourite, but I'm not letting my
heart rule my head at the minute. Bobs Worth has a great big
heart, hasn't he? But I still think Long Run is in there with a
good each-way chance.' He adds: 'It's just a great thing leading
up to it. We work all year for this.'

They do, and we wait all year to see the products of their
hard labour. Yesterday the old chestnut tree that sent pretty
dapples of sunlight down on to the backs of brilliant racehorses
was still barren, but soon it will burst into glorious life again,
and thanks to those brilliant racehorses soon the Festival
will too.

**We know where Sprinter Sacre and Bobs Worth came from,
and just before the Festival Steve Dennis told the story of
how Simonsig came to outstrip his origins in the point-to-
point world beyond all expectations:**

Some horses seem to have that 'X factor', that indefinable
quality that lifts them out of the common herd of bay, grey and

brown and renders them uncommon, unusual, unforgettable.
Simonsig, the hot favourite for next week's Racing Post Arkle
Chase, has the X factor but he also possesses the even rarer
'zero factor', as his owner Ronnie Bartlett explains.

'It was after Simonsig won the big bumper at Fairyhouse
in April 2011,' says Bartlett, managing director of leading
potato suppliers and Cheltenham Festival sponsor
Albert Bartlett.

'When the presentation takes place Ryanair boss Michael
O'Leary plays a game of "deal or no deal" with the winning
owner. He offered me a cheque for €100,000, so I said to him,
"You'll need to put another zero on that." He didn't fancy
doing that.'

There's even a touch of the Kauto Star fairy dust about
the horse, as like Kauto Star the pronunciation of his name
seems to polarise opinion. Simonsig was named by breeder
Simon Tindall, not after himself – 'That would be rather
self-aggrandising, wouldn't it?' Tindall chuckles – but after

Simonsig pictured with Corky (left) and Jerry McGrath, who rides him in most of his fast work. Jerry is one of my fantastic young jockeys, who are all so important to the yard.

a South African wine estate east of Cape Town, and his name is pronounced 'Simmon-sig'.

Time has proved that the potato magnate's valuation of the striking grey was rather shrewder than that of the airline tycoon, yet Simonsig was never originally destined for such giddy heights. It would be a long stretch indeed to suggest that here is a tale of rags to riches, admittedly, but Simonsig has outstripped his origins just as surely as he outstrips the opposition on the racecourse.

'In his younger days I thought he'd be a very smart hunter chaser,' says Nick Pearce, the East Sussex-based point-to-point trainer who breaks in and educates Tindall's young stock.

HENDERSON'S HEROES

'He came here as an unbroken two-year-old, and when I sat on him for the first time at the age of three I honestly felt he'd be decent, although it's terrifying to think back and then forward and realise how much further he's gone.'

Pearce went down the usual route before discovering he had something unusual on his hands.

Simonsig's first appearance on a racecourse was at Penshurst point-to-point in Kent, where Pearce schooled him after racing and where the then iron-grey four-year-old gave his fences plenty of air. He was entered to run at Kingston Blount two weeks later but the ground was too fast and Pearce resolved to put him back in his field and wait another year. He was glad he did.

'I brought him back in at the end of that summer and the transformation was amazing,' he says. 'He'd filled out, he'd become a man, if you like, over the summer.

'So I started working him more, started schooling him, and it soon came to the point where I had to unselfishly say, "He's too good for us." It was the right thing to do to send him to Ireland, because if a horse wins a point-to-point over there it seems to command a much higher price than it would after winning an English point.'

So Simonsig, too good for England, went to be trained by Ian Ferguson in Ballymena, County Antrim. We'll leave him there for a while and go back to the days when Simonsig was no more than a glint in Tindall's mind's eye.

'His dam is a nice mare called Dusty Too, who was trained by Amanda Perrett to win four races for me,' he says.

'Her first foal was an Alflora colt named Clausen, and for her next covering David Minton recommended I send her to Fair Mix, who I'd have to say wouldn't have been the first name on my list. And so we got Simonsig.

'At that time I had four or five potential store horses in the field and he was always much the nicest one. He stood out from the crowd even as a foal – perhaps he's always been a bit of a freak.'

Certainly too freakish for English point-to-points. Tindall has had horses with Ferguson for 20 years, and although Clausen had been sold as a yearling, he too ended up at Ferguson's academy of excellence ... running in the colours of Bartlett. The spheres were beginning to align, beginning to dictate Simonsig's future, the famed triumvirate of Englishman, Irishman and Scotsman coming together for something that would put a smile on so many faces. However, Ferguson's first impressions of the gelding, who was slowly becoming snowier in that endearing way greys have, were less flattering than Tindall might have expected.

'I thought he was a bit of a wimp,' he says. 'He was a bit shy of the foodpot, rather a fussy feeder, and although he took his work well we had to treat him with kid gloves a little bit, just to keep the weight on him.'

Luckily, Simonsig's eating habits were his only drawback. The rest of his repertoire was much more satisfactory and soon had Ferguson purring about his prospects.

'He was a natural athlete from the word go,' he says. 'We soon found that the key to him was not to overwork him, that he didn't need as much work as the other horses.

'But he was gritty, getting braver, and he'd been schooled well by Nick Pearce and certainly wasn't slow about sharpening up his jumping.'

And even though Simonsig made a successful debut in Tindall's blue and yellow colours in a three-mile point-to-point at Kirkistown, County Down, Ferguson's reaction was that of the earnest schoolmaster who demands more from his most promising pupils, with 'could do better' inked redly across the bottom of the race report.

'I was disappointed, to be honest,' he says. 'I know he won, but his jumping was no more than adequate and I expected more because he was working like a very good horse at home.'

Simonsig was ridden on that occasion by Chris Cully, currently enjoying a sabbatical in Australia and who remembers well that first five-finger exercise of this subsequent virtuoso performer. His recollections include the initial mention of a theme upon which all those involved with the horse past and present have their own variations: speed.

'He was like a little motorbike,' says Cully. 'He had unbelievable speed, and although he made a few mistakes on that first run it was mostly down to his being too keen.

'We were all crazy about him at home, everyone liked him and there was nothing they didn't like about him.'

For all his evident speed, Simonsig's course was charted for stamina to begin with. Cully blames that keenness for the 'baby mistake' that sent him sprawling three out at Castletown-Geoghegan on his next start. Ferguson watched from the stands, tearing his hair out and scratching his head at the same time. 'I was wondering what kind of horse he'd be,' he recalls. It was a good question; six days later, next time out, he had the answer.

'Derek O'Connor rode him next time at Limavady and I just told him to ride the horse however he liked, because if he was half the horse I thought he was he'd win easy,' says Ferguson. 'He won by 20 lengths and Derek came back in and said, "This might be the nicest young horse I've ever sat on" – and Derek's ridden plenty of young horses.'

The performance had also caught Bartlett's eye. Poor Clausen had broken a shoulder a fortnight before Simonsig's debut and Bartlett had already sounded out Ferguson about the prospects of the half-brother. Phone calls were made, conversations were had, a deal was done.

'I've known Ronnie for years and I knew he liked Simonsig, and after that victory he asked me if I'd consider selling him,' says Tindall.

'I'm a commercial breeder and I always had it in mind to sell him, especially as I was downsizing a bit at the time, getting on a bit, you see.

'I don't see him as the one that got away, he still seems like my baby, and to breed a Cheltenham Festival winner is the ultimate as far as I'm concerned. Looking back, though, perhaps I should have put a contingency clause in the sale considering what he did next time out!' Two weeks after Bartlett signed the cheque, his new acquisition bounded away from his rivals in the valuable Champion Point-To-Point Bumper at Fairyhouse. It was Simonsig's first run at less than three miles and he showed all the dazzling speed Cully knew he owned.

'When you buy young horses you never know quite what you've got,' says Bartlett, who certainly knew enough to decline O'Leary's offer of a deal missing that crucial zero.

The horse who was too good for English point-to-points was now too good for any point-to-point, too good for bumpers. That autumn Simonsig retraced his steps across the Irish Sea, bound for Nicky Henderson's yard, bound for the top.

'He'd been here a short while and we were just getting going with him,' says Henderson. 'I was talking to Ian and he was quite firm on the point that if I couldn't decide whether to give him one more piece of work or not, the answer should always be "not".

'He might have been a little fragile in those days, not the bravest of the brave, but I'm happy to say he's different now, he's grown up an awful lot, he's much more robust and he's got plenty of self-confidence.'

His new sturdier nature was displayed to sparkling effect this winter, when he won two novice chases within seven days at Ascot and Kempton, an imposition Henderson wouldn't dream of setting a horse with a lesser constitution. And the theme of speed sustains.

'Enormous speed,' says Henderson. Regular rider Barry Geraghty chooses the refinement of 'so much pace', echoing Cully's sentiments. Simonsig in full cry is a thrill to watch and it's no surprise to find that he's just as much fun to ride.

'He jumps brilliantly, he's better over fences than he was over hurdles,' says Geraghty, the practice his partner gained from Penshurst to Limavady making near-perfect.

'He's got a lovely attitude, he settles, he travels, he's so straightforward and he's so versatile. He has the pace for two miles and stays three miles well – it gives him all the options.'

The keenness Cully mentioned is still part of Simonsig's armoury although Henderson has learned how to defuse it, ensuring that he blows off a bit of steam before he starts schooling just to take the edge off his raw enthusiasm. 'Last time we schooled him he had two bloody good canters beforehand, and it wouldn't hurt him to gallop before going over his fences either,' he says.

The regime is working wonders and bore Festival fruit in last year's Neptune Investment Novices' Hurdle. For Bartlett, who had won the Foxhunter the previous year with Zemsky and who has Simonsig's half-brother Simarthur in training

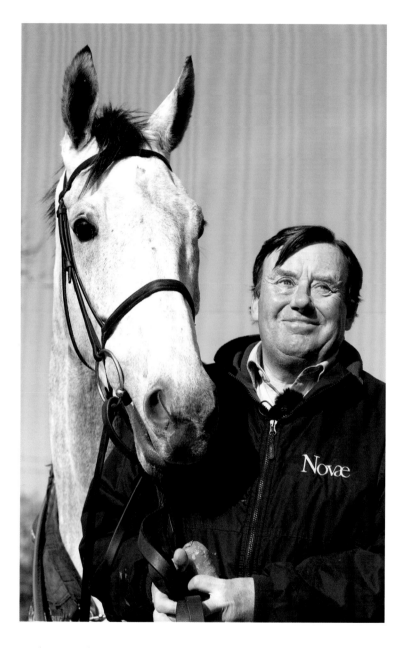

This really should be a potato, and not a carrot, that I'm giving to Simonsig. Ronnie Bartlett does supply us with potatoes, but a few years ago he asked if we wanted a few carrots and I said I did. However, I was surprised when a low loader appeared with ten tonnes. I could have schooled the horses during the night!

with Lucinda Russell, it was the high point in 30 years of owning racehorses.

'What a dream, back-to-back wins at the Festival,' he says, and when pressed on the likelihood of an even dreamier hat-trick in the Arkle responds with the caution of a man who knows racing and horses well, careful to make the caveat that it's much more than a two-horse race.

Simonsig and Barry (centre) lead the Neptune Novices' Hurdle field at the 2012 Cheltenham Festival as Cotton Mill crashes out at the second last. It will be fascinating to see how far he gets in time, but you have to be to able to stay to win a Neptune.

'He might be one of those horses with enough class and options that we don't have to worry about which race he runs in or who the opposition are. I know horses don't last all that long at the top and you've got to make the most of every minute.'

He's certainly getting his 60 seconds' worth out of Simonsig, whose rare versatilty – another echo of Kauto Star, perhaps – gives his connections an ace up every sleeve. Two miles next year? Three miles? The Gold Cup? 'If we start taking on Sprinter Sacre over two miles it would be interesting to see which one Barry would ride,' grins Bartlett, not knowing that Geraghty had already made his feelings plain when wondering aloud about running the Queen Mother Champion Chase in two divisions.

Henderson has been widely quoted as saying Simonsig has the speed to be placed in a Champion Hurdle, but falls a little way short of recommending his Gold Cup chances. 'If he stayed the Gold Cup trip he'd be utterly unbeatable because he's got so much toe,' he says. 'He'd be a freak,

One high point in the build-up to Cheltenham, which was not directly related to the Festival itself, was the victory of Close Touch – owned by Her Majesty the Queen – in the EBF Novices' Hurdle Final at Sandown with Barry on board.

but I don't expect I'll get the chance to find out the answer to that question.'

That all lies ahead, beyond the bright horizon of next Tuesday. The sky is the limit for Simonsig; Bartlett and everyone else involved in the fairytale are already on cloud nine.

THE CHELTENHAM FESTIVAL

Previous spread: Simonsig and Barry clear the last in the 2013 Racing Post Arkle at Cheltenham.

OF COURSE IT'S NICE to have lots of the favourites for the Festival, although it obviously intensifies the pressure. You wouldn't swap it for not having such good horses. We struggled a bit with Oscar Whisky and Finian's Rainbow (who never once got the ground he needs), but the rest of the team was strong in quality and quantity.

We always have something of a houseful for Cheltenham – in 2013 Jessie Harrington stayed (but Johnny sadly didn't as he was unwell – though he made our end-of-season party), Michael Buckley stayed, there were quite a few here for the four days. We had seven winners the year before but I would always settle for one on the first day because that takes the pressure off.

I thought My Tent Or Yours, who ran in the Supreme Novices' Hurdle on the opening day, was a seriously good bumper horse, and one morning in the autumn AP was schooling him by chance and he said, 'The only problem with this one is that he runs in the wrong colours'. AP talked to JP and he bought him, but I felt a bit sorry for the bunch of mates who owned him.

I don't know where all the buzz about the Champion Hurdle came from – he was always going to run in the Supreme and he didn't win that as he finished second to Champagne Fever, so it's just as well he didn't go for the Champion.

Next up on day one was Simonsig, who is 100 per cent in every way but does have a slight propensity to get 'mucky lungs', and he suffered from that in January, which is why he didn't run between the second of his two quick novice chase wins and the Festival. He's terribly easy to get ready.

Three weeks before Cheltenham he was in scintillating form – we could have changed our minds and put him in the Champion Hurdle and I still reckon he'd have won it. Sometime in the last week before the Festival Jerry thought he might have lost a bit of his spark, but nothing was tangibly wrong.

Coming down the hill at Cheltenham in the Arkle he looked as though he'd win well, but he was 'messy' when he came back and things had obviously caught up with him again. He usually settles very well but we knew something must have been wrong because all he wanted to do was push on, but we were off and running for the Festival. Lee Mottershead reported on the race for the *Post:*

CHELTENHAM

MARCH 12, 2013

Racing Post Arkle Challenge Trophy Chase 2m

1 Simonsig 8-15f
Barry Geraghty

2 Baily Green 33-1
David Casey

3 His Excellency 80-1
Tom Scudamore

Distances 2¼l, 13l

What many considered the inevitable outcome duly materialised, if not in the manner expected. Yet although some connected with Simonsig perhaps seemed underwhelmed by the style of his victory, they have an excellent winner of the Racing Post Arkle Chase, a fearsome talent for whom an even greater assignment may now be as inevitable as yesterday's outcome.

Talk of a match-up with the gallant Overturn there might have been, but odds of 8-15 confirmed this was Simonsig's race to lose. He pulled far too hard and then engaged in an untimely disagreement with a back-straight fence. But the race was not lost, and one of the fastest chasers ever to cross Cheltenham's hallowed turf remains a star for today whose tomorrow appears increasingly certain to involve a meeting with the outstanding stablemate whose illustrious path he was yesterday following.

True, a driven-out two-and-a-quarter-length defeat of 33-1 outsider Baily Green does not match up to the Sprinter Sacre tour de force of 2012, but the difficulties Simonsig imposed upon himself – not to mention the slightly crestfallen reaction of those closest to him – leaves you convinced there is better to come. And should he ever lock horns with today's Champion Chase favourite, better will be needed.

'He got the job done, even if some of it wasn't as pretty as you would have liked,' said Nicky Henderson, who had trained Ronnie Bartlett's grey to win last year's Neptune Investment Management Novices' Hurdle.

'He was always doing a little too much early on. He wasn't concentrating as you would have liked, but he was quick in and out of his fences, even if sometimes he wasn't the tidiest.

'He does look like a two-miler through and through and he'd certainly be hard to hold over two and a half. How would you stop him? We'll work out what to do next season when it comes, but both he and Sprinter Sacre look like two-milers.'

Simonsig's next chance to show how good a two-miler he could be will very probably come at Aintree, where Barry Geraghty might expect more than what he yesterday described as 'a good, stout performance'.

Geraghty reflected: 'Maybe he was a bit fresh and got himself on edge. I suppose I thought he would have found it easier to travel, but he was very free and made a mistake down the back, so things were stacked against him, and enough to beat most horses.'

Although all out at the finish, Simonsig had more than enough to beat Baily Green, who nevertheless delighted trainer Mouse Morris.

'I'm not being cocky but I'm not surprised how well he ran,' said Morris, while Overturn's trainer Donald McCain – whose popular front-runner finished one place behind third home His Excellency, having lost momentum with a mistake three fences out – lamented conditions that proved just too gruelling.

'It was the ground,' said McCain. 'It's tacky and holding out there, which is no good for him. Jason [Maguire] said he never gave him the usual feel.'

Nor did Simonsig give Geraghty the usual feel, but despite what Bartlett called 'a nerve-wracking experience' he won, which meant the potato magnate, Henderson and Geraghty received their precious prizes from Racing Post guest Denise Lewis, one of the great all-round athletes.

In the belief Simonsig could also be an all-rounder, Boylesports make him 10-1 for next year's Champion Hurdle, 12-1 for the Gold Cup and 6-1 for the Champion Chase.

But, if Henderson is correct, Simonsig is not an all-rounder. Like Sprinter Sacre, he could be an exceptional one-trick pony. At some thrilling point next season we may find out which of the Seven Barrows superstars executes that trick best.

In the Champion Hurdle Binocular could finish only fifth behind impressive winner Hurricane Fly, while Grandouet

Rajdhani Express and Sam take the novice handicap chase to bring up an opening day double, which always takes the pressure off despite what is still to come. This was a seriously good performance off top weight and he is still improving.

was going well before falling four flights from home. The day ended on a high note, though, when Rajdhani Express won the Rewards4Racing Novices' Handicap Chase. David Carr reported:

Not a bad start to a potentially momentous week. Become a father on Sunday. Ride your fourth Cheltenham Festival winner on Tuesday. Now Sam Waley-Cohen just needs to recapture the Gold Cup on Friday to complete the set.

Two days after his wife Annabel gave birth to baby Max, the amateur rider warmed up for Long Run's date with destiny by landing the Rewards4Racing Novices' Handicap Chase on top-weight Rajdhani Express, holding Ackertac off by a neck.

'It has been magical,' he said. 'Now I'll go home to my wife and new baby and watch the replays. Everyone at home said, "Go and do it", so I came here off not much sleep and it has all worked out.'

The winner is trained by Nicky Henderson, who said: 'He has jumped great. When he won at Kempton over Christmas he

CHELTENHAM

MARCH 12, 2013

Rewards4Racing Novices'
Handicap Chase 2m 4½f

1 Rajdhani Express   16-1
Mr Sam Waley-Cohen

2 Ackertac   66-1
Sam Twiston-Davies

3 Ohio Gold   16-1
Joe Tizzard

4 Shangani   6-1
Aidan Coleman

Distances nk, 9l, 1¾l

looked like he was going to be a good horse. The handicapper gave him a mighty belt and we came here in January and it was very soft. He wasn't the same horse.

'But this shows that some of this ground is not riding too bad. They've done a brilliant job here, to get this ground as good as it is.'

Rajdhani Express is owned by the jockey's father Robert, who is also Cheltenham chairman. He said: 'He's my first homebred winner at the Festival, so that's a huge pleasure. With Sam riding it, and having had a baby on Sunday, what could be better?' The winning owner added: 'Rajdhani won on Boxing Day and then Long Run won, so I hope this is a good omen.'

The highlight of day two was Sprinter Sacre and I couldn't believe the amount of people who had gathered around the saddling boxes in the pre-parade ring just to catch a glimpse of him. I've never seen a crowd like it.

He was absolutely 100 per cent there, right at his very peak. The Champion Chase is *it*, the race of the season. Barry said he was 100 per cent there, then at Aintree he was probably 95 per cent, and at Punchestown he was 85 per cent. They can't stay at an absolute peak for six weeks, it's impossible.

It's an absolute joy to look at something like him every morning and every night – but when he's racing he does terrify me. When they went down to the start for the Champion Chase Minty and I walked out to our manhole cover, whereupon the racecourse announcer said, 'Four and a half minutes to post time', and I found myself standing there with my heart going bang, bang, bang. I thought, 'I can't stand here for four and a half minutes' – it was terrifying.

I suppose that's the bargain you strike with a horse like that. When he gets beat the whole world will descend upon me. Barry says it's spectacular fun. I say, 'Well I'm glad you're enjoying it, old boy.' I hate every second of it. It's no fun. It's scary. But as long as everyone else is enjoying it, I'll do the sweating. Graham Dench reported on a spectacular victory:

Sprinter Sacre and Barry saunter home in the Queen Mother Champion Chase. I think this was the day we could finally admit he was a champion.

Nothing short of sensational would have sufficed, and Sprinter Sacre was nothing short of sensational.

Nicky Henderson was a bundle of nerves and described watching the race unfold as 'hell', but for the rest of us it was among the most sublime experiences we have been privileged to witness on a racecourse.

The 19 lengths by which Sprinter Sacre scored was by no means the Queen Mother Champion Chase's widest winning margin – Master Minded scored by an identical distance as recently as 2008 and former greats such as Dunkirk, Crisp and Badsworth Boy all won by even further – but surely none of them treated yardsticks as talented as 2011 winner Sizing Europe with quite such disdain.

Following another virtually flawless display, Sprinter Sacre simply sauntered away from Sizing Europe approaching the final bend, the pair of them having already left classy rivals standing as they started down the hill.

Sportingbet Queen Mother
Champion Chase 2m

1 Sprinter Sacre   1-4f
Barry Geraghty

2 Sizing Europe   6-1
Andrew Lynch

3 Wishfull Thinking   25-1
Richard Johnson

Distances 19l, 6l

The winner was never remotely off the bridle and, while only time will tell, one cannot help thinking the hastily calculated 188 revealed by BHA head of handicapping Phil Smith – still 5lb short of Kauto Star's peak – may well turn out to seriously underestimate him. The Racing Post Rating of 190 is the highest figure ever record at the Festival.

Barry Geraghty, who enjoyed a superb association with dual Champion Chase winner Moscow Flyer, was reluctant to make comparisons, but admitted that while Moscow Flyer was 'a super horse', Sprinter Sacre is 'just unbelievable and oozes class'.

'I've never ridden a horse that does it all so easily,' he added. 'He's like Pele, who used to do it all so easily because his speed and power and skill gave him the time to do it.'

He is only seven and yet to be troubled in eight starts over fences and we can look forward to one more sight of Sprinter Sacre this year, in the Champion Chase at Punchestown. And then a year from now we have the tantalising prospect of a head-to-head with stablemate Simonsig.

Paddy Power make Sprinter Sacre a 4-6 chance for the 2014 Queen Mother, with Simonsig at 6-1, but he is even shorter elsewhere, the race sponsor going 1-3, and Henderson also has the 2012 winner Finian's Rainbow to throw back into the mix.

'That was probably the worst five minutes of my life, but so long as Barry enjoyed it that's great,' said Henderson as he waited for Sprinter Sacre to return to the winner's enclosure.

'That's a proper racehorse, doing what steeplechasing is all about. He's got that wow factor about him, and he knows it too. What he looks like and what he does at home is one thing, but what he does out there is totally unique.'

Originally bought as part of a 'job lot' of 21 by David Minton for owners Raymond and Caroline Mould, and fortuitously for Seven Barrows sent to Henderson when they were dispersed among four trainers, Sprinter Sacre has evidently always displayed extraordinary natural talent.

Henderson said: 'He doesn't hide his light under a bushel and he doesn't do anything by halves. He knows he's good and he likes to tell everyone. He's almost the perfect racehorse. We are very lucky to have him. It's a true privilege.'

Barry had obviously enjoyed himself and I think, and hope, the crowd did too. The reception was about as vociferous as I can remember. To owner Caroline Mould and me it was a huge relief, but at the same time an honour for us both to be connected with a horse who has captured the hearts of the racing world.

He added: 'I'm sure he'll get further, but would you ever dare ask him? He could easily go to Punchestown, because he's had only three races this season, then I think he'd follow a similar programme next season.'

Henderson agreed it would be hard to keep Sprinter Sacre and Simonsig apart, but said: 'If they meet, they meet – it's Barry who's going to have the problem.'

Sizing Europe beat the rest decisively, despite a scare when he lost his hind legs crossing the woodchip path after the third-last.

Jockey Andrew Lynch confirmed he tripped but admitted: 'The race was over and I couldn't use that as an excuse. Sprinter Sacre is some horse. It was worth taking a shot at him to find out how good he is, and it just shows you that he really is a proper horse. My lad still ran well.'

Trainer Henry de Bromhead was as proud of Sizing Europe as he was unstinting in his praise of the winner, who he said was 'phenomenal'.

He added: 'We'll see if we come back next year. Our horse was still second in a Champion Chase with some good horses behind him. He's still good. It was the right decision to run. We did everything to go out to win the race and I thought he jumped brilliantly. He did everything brilliantly and was just beaten by a very special horse on the day.'

Alastair Down watched in wonder a performance of awesome power and immense class from Sprinter Sacre:

Just before half past three yesterday afternoon the map of the known jumping world was redrawn forever when Sprinter Sacre took the sport into hitherto uncharted territory with a gasp-inducing masterclass the like of which has never previously been seen over two miles of fast-flown steeplechase fences.

Rarely has the Festival air crackled with such anticipatory excitement as in the minutes during which the field made its way out to parade before the purist's ultimate examination that is the Champion Chase. And it is almost impossible to convey how awesome Sprinter Sacre looked – coat gleaming like a polished mahogany table, all power and muscle coiled under Geraghty and, most extraordinary of all, with an air of pure threat and lethality about him.

There is something almost scary about Sprinter Sacre, something not quite suitable for the children. To this increasingly seasoned observer he is the first X-rated chaser.

As the seconds ticked away to off-time, debate on the press balcony concluded that what we wanted to see was Sprinter Scare win by at least 15 lengths and for the admirable Sizing Europe to finish second, thus giving the necessary degree of gold-plating to the form.

The moment of revelation came as they began the descent of the hill. Suddenly the two central characters in the drama simply ghosted 15 lengths clear, the issue between them alone and the chaff blown away to a zone of utter irrelevance.

Sprinter Sacre was upsides Sizing Europe three from and then there came one of those marvellous moments when pure class cut in and he eased clear. It was not some dramatic quickening or the result of Barry Geraghty doing anything as impertinent as asking him to go to work – it was just the race-changing exertion of his incalculable superiority.

Five lengths clear two out, he simply processed away, the king coming to his coronation and his admiring subjects in the stands unleashed a crashing adulatory roar – tens of thousands of voices speaking as one – as he touched down, safe, secure and supreme on the landing side of the last.

Still barely doing more than go through the motions and never under the slightest pressure, he stretched 19 unforgettable lengths clear up the run-in leaving the abiding impression that despite having annihilated his field there was any amount still in untapped reserve.

Many of those who pack the Cheltenham enclosures at the Festival do so in the fervent hope it will be during their time, on their watch, that horses of genuine wonder will come along and change forever our idea of the possible. Sprinter Sacre did just that yesterday and the reception he received from the faithful as he and Geraghty came back down the horse walk mingled admiration with excitement and no small touch of awe.

The awaiting winner's enclosure was under siege with the steppings rammed by those wanting to feast their eyes on this new force of sporting nature. There was a curiously muted air as we waited for Geraghty to bring him in, with voices fractionally lowered like a congregation in church.

As the conquerors reached half way up the paddock through that funnel of folk to where the real fans await, the noise of acclaim built and long and loud were the cheers as he made his way into the spot he occupied after the Racing Post Arkle last year and to which he has seemed destined to return ever since.

The crowd at Cheltenham after the Champion Chase were absolutely fantastic.

It wasn't an Irish reception, or one of those joyful riots that mark the return of some winners: there was a degree of relief that it was over and that dreams of future afternoons of the incredible were happily intact.

Power is what this horse is about, but it is no longer raw power. Henderson's tutelage, Corky Browne's grizzled wisdom, Nico de Boinville's sympathetic hands and Geraghty's flawless execution have fettled an increasingly mature marvel who is still only seven. Henderson summed it up: 'It's all about his build, balance and brain – he can work it all out.'

And barely had the sweat dried on him than the official handicappers rushed out Sprinter Sacre's new vital statistic – they had raised him from 179 to 188, officially the best two-mile chaser of the modern era.

Since the Champion Chase was first run in 1959 ten horses have won it twice, and just Badsworth Boy three times. When Master Minded won his first Champion Chase every bit as impressively at the age of five in 2008 it looked as if he would reap a similar harvest, but though he won the following year he never again quite knocked the eye out in the same fashion.

Yesterday Barry Geraghty, the man who made Moscow fly, rightly pointed out that new superlatives may have to be minted to describe Sprinter Sacre, but he used a wonderfully incisive term when he said the horse 'struts' his way through races and there is plenty of swagger about this fearsome-looking beast.

More years will be needed to establish his exact place in the jumps firmament but he is a shooting star and who knows to what places he may yet take us.

We didn't have a winner on the third day, which was overshadowed by the dreadful fall that John Thomas McNamara suffered in the Kim Muir Chase. The news that JT had suffered a serious neck injury, which left him paralysed, affected everyone, not least JP McManus, for whom he rode so many winners.

It was a brave shout to go straight to the Gold Cup with Bobs Worth, a calculated risk. It was the lesser of the two evils, because if we'd run him on that heavy ground in the spring we'd have most likely banjaxed him for the Festival. We had to do a lot of work with him, and that's not my natural position. He was working very well and we took him for a spin round Kempton, but we had to keep at him.

The crucial part is if you have one person who is top-class and rides a horse every day – Shane Gribbin does that with Bobs Worth. They can tell you so much and there is no substitute for that, and because Bobs Worth has highs and lows Shane is crucial to him.

I was very happy with Long Run before the Gold Cup, and although the last few pieces of work Bobs Worth did were among the best I'd seen him do, I was also mindful that he'd only had one race out of novice company. That's quite a big gulf to be crossed.

Nothing will give me greater pleasure than winning that Gold Cup for some great people, some great mates … to do it for them was wonderful. The passion they have for their racing is almost unimaginable, and knowing how much pleasure it gave them means an awful lot to me. Jon Lees reported on this extra-special victory for Seven Barrows:

Betfred Cheltenham Gold
Cup 3m 2½f

1 Bobs Worth   11-4f
Barry Geraghty

2 Sir Des Champs   4-1
AP McCoy

3 Long Run   7-2
Mr Sam Waley-Cohen

Distances 7l, 2¾l

Every successful double act has a straight guy and after capturing the Champion Chase with Sprinter Sacre, Nicky Henderson secured the Betfred Cheltenham Gold Cup yesterday with Bobs Worth, a horse who is the antithesis of his showman stablemate.

While Sprinter Sacre drew all the rave reviews, Bobs Worth had shunned the limelight for 104 days until, without the benefit of a dress rehearsal, he stepped back on to jump racing's biggest stage and delivered the performance of the complete professional.

Henderson, who saddled first and third, secured his 50th Cheltenham Festival victory as Bobs Worth beat Irish Hennessy winner Sir Des Champs by seven lengths, with Long Run, the 2011 Gold Cup hero and dual King George winner, two and three quarters of a length behind. The Giant Bolster, runner-up a year ago, was fourth this time.

The Not Afraid Partnership of longstanding Henderson supporters – Malcolm Kimmins, John Jarvis, Caro Wells, Nick Deacon and David Nash – had never seen Bobs Worth defeated in four appearances at Cheltenham, a record jockey Barry Geraghty was determined to protect.

There was a moment when, with Long Run setting the pace approaching three out, Bobs Worth appeared to lose touch with the principals. However, Geraghty didn't give up and when Silviniaco Conti crashed out they were soon back in the race and once they grabbed the lead approaching the last the outcome was sealed.

Whenever he has hit the front Bobs Worth has never been headed and, valiantly as the others tried, he was too strong for his opponents as he became the first horse since Flyingbolt to win three difference Festival races.

'The stat that came into my head between the last two was that once this horse gets his head in front he hasn't been headed and I was praying it wasn't going to be today,' said Geraghty.

'Between five and six out I was in trouble and I knew jumping three out that they had got six or seven lengths clear of me. But they weren't getting any further and I could feel my fellow was filling up. So I just nursed him and nursed him and didn't go for everything. I was driving in fourth gear and saving fifth gear until the second-last.'

Bobs Worth and Barry (centre) battle for Gold Cup glory with Sir Des Champs and AP (left); Long Run and Sam are just behind in third. Bobs' low head carriage shows how incredibly hard he tries – he just puts his head down and fights and fights and fights. This hill was built for him and the Gold Cup was the fifth time he had defeated it.

Since winning last year's RSA Chase Bobs Worth had run only once, re-emerging on December 1 to capture the Hennessy Gold Cup before retreating into an unscheduled winter hibernation as a warm-up in the Argento Chase in January was scrapped because of heavy ground.

Henderson, who appears assured of his first trainers' championship since 1986–87, said: 'We took a rather odd preparation with Bobs Worth and Long Run. They haven't run since the Hennessy and King George and to get them here is a huge effort.

'Bobs Worth came into this much better than he did when he won the RSA. I'd had a terrible winter with him then and I just didn't want to go through that again. I was going to run him here in January but the ground was horrible. A hard race in that would have been tough. If he'd run there I'd have had no horse to prepare for March.

'When Sam was having a head-to-head with AP, Bobs Worth was out of the picture and I more or less thought he was out of the race. But then Minty grabbed me by the neck and said, 'Bobs is coming, he's coming'. From there I was pretty confident. He's nothing flashy but very professional, like the man on top.

'I was very lucky to win the championship before, but then it was post-Dickinson and pre-Pipe when there was a gap of about two years and there was room for somebody. We were always in the first five or six, but in the last couple of years we've had better horses. It got quite tight last year and we've still got Aintree, but it would be great to get it back.'

Kimmins was elated. 'I thought we weren't going to get there and then I thought we would be in the first three, which would have been amazing,' he said. 'Then he pulls it out again and I don't know where he gets it from. They were tired at the end.

'I was surrounded by my two daughters and a son, my sister and wife and a few other followers and they held me together. We've all been loyal supporters with Nicky. I had horses with Fulke Walwyn, but nothing like this. It's just an amazing experience that you dream of. I still can't quite believe it. It is true, is it?'

Although Geraghty enjoyed his second Gold Cup victory – he also won in 2005 on Kicking King – with a horse he had bought as a yearling for €16,500 and sold on for £20,000 three years later, his thoughts were with John Thomas McNamara.

'It's one of the biggest days of my career, but all I can think about is a good friend of ours in hospital,' he said. 'I'll dedicate this to him if it's any good, but we all just want him to be okay.'

Alastair Down witnessed a chaser with substance power to victory and provide me with a 50th Festival success:

It remains a mystery where Barry Geraghty goes off and hides on Bobs Worth mid-race, but you can set your watch by the fact this stealth bomber of a chaser will turn up at the muck and bullets end to blow away his rivals, and he did exactly that to grab a gruelling Cheltenham Gold Cup yesterday.

With Long Run setting off in front to bring his grinding qualities into play, this was a no-hiding-place race from

With Bobs Worth in the winner's enclosure after the Gold Cup. I'd forgotten what a dreadfully wet day it was, but you do forget at times like this. It had been a great week, and to finish it with the Gold Cup and a 50th Festival winner were jewels in the crown.

the start and Sir Des Champs was on the leader's coattails throughout with Ruby Walsh never worse than handy on Silviniaco Conti, who made light of a mistake on the first circuit and travelled well looking full of threat.

As they went to the top of the hill for the second time Bobs Worth actually nosed into third up the rail, but between six and five out he suddenly seemed to be labouring and dropped back to sixth place with the writing seemingly on the wall and Geraghty subsequently admitted he thought he was beat.

But you have to remember what a boot-tough little nugget you are dealing with here. Twice before he has been to the forcing ground of the Festival and twice returned to Seven Barrows triumphant and there is no fight too savage for him.

Going to the third-last he still had seven lengths to find on Long Run and Sir Des Champs and it was here that Silviniaco Conti, still going conspicuously strongly, fell. Bobs Worth had the agility to step round him and the game was still in play.

At this stage Geraghty had a good six lengths to make up but the race was entering the pain zone and whereas most horses are broken on the wheel of this desperate old hill to Bobs Worth it almost seems to act as a spur because the climb to the summit holds no fears for him.

On the run to the second-last Sir Des Champs and Long Run were beginning to flounder and Bobs Worth had 'em now, reeling in the front two with every head-down stride. Fractionally in third two out, he threw in a terrific jump and by now the stands were erupting for the favourite as, in terms of reserves, they could see he was the last man standing and had just the final fence between him and the Gold Cup.

He landed running but somehow AP got a last big leap from Sir Des Champs who, though patently past the end of his tether, staged a rally that was nothing short of magnificent. Running on no more than instinct, he wrenched back Bobs Worth's lead to a length and a half, but 70 yards from the line he literally had no more to give and the winner just powered on and had stretched his superiority to seven lengths at the line.

I wrote yesterday that Bobs Worth 'is like the faceless assassin in the crowd – you don't know he is there until he steps into the limelight and delivers the coup de grace' and his manner of victory lived up to that billing exactly but it is already time to re-evaluate his stature.

Sold for £20,000 – just a 'bob's worth' – he is the 'nothing horse' who has turned out to be everything. Geraghty produced a beautifully telling line yesterday when he said Bobs Worth 'impersonates a workmanlike horse but is much more than that'. I know I couldn't do Barry's job but it's clear he could do mine!

And this is a chaser of very real substance. He is the first horse since the savage but brilliant Flyingbolt, stablemate of Arkle, to win three different races at the Cheltenham Festival and you can't keep higher company than that.

He is not purely about stamina and durability. Geraghty said that in his final racecourse gallop at Kempton he showed that bit of boot the really good ones have to have as part of their repertoire.

And a word must be said about Nicky Henderson, who chose the Gold Cup as the stage on which to produce his 50th Festival winner and brought Bobs Worth here in the form of his lifetime after a 104-day break since his Hennessy win.

Henderson, 28 years on from his first Festival win, said 'we've been very lucky here' to which one can only reply 'twaddle'. Henderson's Cheltenham haul has been built by many hands – most notably those of the ageless Corky

Browne, but it is Henderson who is the orchestrator of the achievement. Luck is an incidental, talent verging on genius with jumpers is immutable.

Usually with the excitement of the Gold Cup and the teeming atmosphere of this incomparable meeting the thoughts of those on course tend not to stray elsewhere. But not on this day.

Throughout the afternoon titans of the sport such as JP McManus, AP McCoy and Geraghty spoke as one in their moments of triumph about John Thomas McNamara and how any feelings of happiness were alien to this hour.

The weighing room is peopled by men of flint who are bound by steel bands of comradeship. They live with appalling danger as an everyday commonplace and, of course, they can not afford to dwell on the risk. But cut them and they bleed just like the rest of us and there can have been very few occasions in my lifetime when the weighing room has felt a blow so shatteringly.

Jump racing looks after its own and rises to the occasion most brilliantly when things are at their grimmest. That McNamara will lack for nothing in terms of care and resource is simply not even a shred of consolation.

At the end of this Festival week it is impossible to depart with anything else in your mind than the figure who left here in the air ambulance at the irredeemably bleak end of Thursday afternoon.

We decided to invite everyone to the Barrows on the Friday evening. Bobs Worth's owners were there and Johnny Worrall came back. The jockeys have their own party in the weighing room at Cheltenham – the sort of thing trainers are not invited to! The morning after Rodney Masters joined the celebrations:

One must applaud the Bronze Age Lambourn residents of 4,000 years ago for their foresight in naming Seven Barrows in honour of Nicky Henderson's seven winners at Cheltenham 2012 AD.

Clearly their wise chief, most probably a relative of Tom Segal, *Racing Post*'s Pricewise tipster, was blessed with another vision because excited archaeologists have now discovered around 50 barrows in the immediate vicinity. That's one for every Henderson Festival winner.

Where those old-timers seriously let us down was when failing to allocate individual names to the barrows in honour of the stable's Festival multi-achievers, such as See You Then, The Tsarevich, Remittance Man, Stormyfairweather, Simonsig, Bobs Worth and Sprinter Sacre.

Breakfast time yesterday at the stables witnessed a joyful mix of old and new faces to fanfare the four latest Festival heroes – the newest face being that of Henderson's first grandchild, babe-in-arms Harry Giffard, the son of middle daughter Tessa, who was on his first public day out.

Photographers asked the trainer to put down the Gold Cup and pick up his grandson. Henderson looked more nervous than at any time in a week when he was caught on Channel 4 cameras doing Group-class nerves most afternoons. He declined, saying: 'I'm frightened enough of dropping the Gold Cup. I'd be terrified of dropping Harry.'

In the background was one of the more weathered faces, though one that never dropped its wide smile. Malcolm Kimmins is a former many things, including a Newbury racecourse director for eight years, a whisky company representative and then a wine merchant. His deep passion for jump racing is on a par with that of JP McManus and has never wilted since he first had horses in training with Fulke Walwyn more than 50 years ago.

Known affectionately as Kimbo, he lives in the Lambourn Valley. Throughout the region and its environs there is jubilation beyond measure that this jovial character, who would tell of his repeated dream of owning a Gold Cup winner, has now done so. He heads up the Not Afraid Partnership, which includes another racecourse executive, John Jarvis.

Kimmins told of a long night when he displayed Bobs Worth's reserves of stamina, saying: 'We got back to the yard and had a little celebration. At 3am I had another whisky and watched the race again. And then again. There wasn't much sleep, if any. Too excited for that.'

His first horse was Misty Isle. 'He looked like a greyhound and I was surprised Fulke allowed him in the yard,' remembers Kimmins. 'He tended not to like that type.

The morning after the week that was: the press descended first thing on Saturday morning and we were all ready but a bit bleary-eyed. Here I am pictured with my daughters Camilla (left), Tessa, holding my ten-week old grandson Harry, and Sarah – and, of course, Bobs Worth.

Simonsig, Bobs Worth and Sprinter Sacre all returned safe and sound, which was the most important thing.

The work doesn't stop just because you've had a successful Cheltenham Festival! It was now time to start plotting our moves for the final part of the season.

'I'd a good one called Zellaman, who would have won the Schweppes [Betfair Hurdle] but for falling. Fulke fancied him. That's the only time I've been physically sick on a racecourse; it was all too much for me.

'Most of the horses were shared with my brother-in-law Christopher Pilkington, but he didn't take a share in Bobs Worth because at the time he'd just bought another one. We'd always talked of winning the Gold Cup together. He was at Cheltenham, bless him. It must have hurt not to be involved.'

Bobs Worth is looked after by Tomas Dolezal, 36, tall enough to look John Gosden in the eye and who therefore makes the Gold Cup winner look smaller than the reality when at his head.

His English is improving, but is not quite there yet. However, he manages to tell us he was a baker in his home town of Trencin, Slovakia, and that he came to Lambourn seven years ago via Israel, where he was a gardener.

Under his care he also has River Maigue and Master Of The Hall and has additional responsibilities as a yardman. His English improves when he talks of his unshakable belief in a horse who never knows when he is beaten. 'Of course I backed Bobs Worth,' he says. 'He was always going to win. I had on £1,000.'

Team Seven Barrows celebrated in The Blowing Stone at Kingston Lisle. 'We were there until 3am and then up again at 5.30am,' said Danni Loader, whose charge Kid Cassidy finished runner-up in the Johnny Henderson Grand Annual. For Loader there was no time for an afternoon snooze. She was off to Kempton to lead up two.

When the media had drifted away yesterday, there was a special moment for me, courtesy of Corky Browne.

Corky took me for a private audience with Sprinter Sacre. The pin-up horse Henderson has nicknamed James Bond – 'he'd be the one invited to all the smart parties and always be seen talking to the prettiest girl in nightclubs but would always be at the top of his profession the next day' – is stabled away from the main yard. The horse without a flaw is in a far-end box.

We both remember Tom Dreaper's Flyingbolt and agree Sprinter is in the same league. Straightening Sprinter's rugs, Corky explains why he is in this box. 'He was in the main yard but he found that all too busy and he'd walk his box,' he reveals. 'Up here he's fine. When the weather is good the big doors adjacent to his box are open and he loves that.'

Asked if he had considered retirement, he grins: 'How can anyone retire from a job like mine when we've horses about like this one, Bobs Worth, Simonsig and Captain Conan?'

For the last two years, Sophie and I have escaped on the Saturday after Cheltenham for a few days with the Hanburys to their lovely retreat in St Moritz, along with the Kelvin Hugheses and Barry and Penny Hills. It's great, because going into the week you can say, 'Whatever happens, we can get away from it all on Saturday.' And we don't do a lot of skiing. I saw first lot out and made sure the runners for the day were all sorted before we left.

On the Saturday afternoon Barry and myself were climbing up to St Moritz on a train trying to listen to a commentary of the bumper at Kempton, where I had a runner and Barry's son Charlie had one as well. Barry fancied theirs and I fancied mine, but I didn't let on. West Wizard won for Seven Barrows by six lengths and the Hills horse finished ninth!

AINTREE AND PUNCHESTOWN – AND ROYAL ASCOT

AINTREE IS GOOD FUN and is completely different from Cheltenham in that it is more relaxed. We stay with Bobby McAlpine, who had 1986 Supreme Novices' Hurdle winner River Ceiriog with us, and his wife Angela, and unlike Cheltenham, when we come back every night to Seven Barrows, we are away from the yard for all three days. The last three years there have been fantastic, but before we got to Aintree Rodney Masters talked to Corky Browne about the horses and men who have defined his career:

Little surprise Nicky Henderson's legendary first lieutenant Corky Browne required replacement knees. On his feet for most of every day as he darts between yards and in and out of boxes at Seven Barrows, he has clocked 272,160 miles, give or take a few. He has probably run a hand down a couple of million tendons.

Browne pushes back his cap and grins. 'They strapped one of those pedometers to my left leg for a day. It clocked 27 miles,' he says. 'That surprised me, but after giving it some thought it was probably accurate enough. I'm on the go from 5am until 6.30 or 7pm, apart from lunchtime. My right knee is giving me a bit of discomfort, but with all these good horses about the place the pain disappears.

'Funny that. It's the same with this cold wind. It's been a long and difficult winter, yet it doesn't seem to matter because we've always so much to look forward to.'

Henderson's first recruit 35 years ago, Browne will be 71 in June, but is not for abdication as head lad. His eyes sparkle with boyish enthusiasm when he talks of his elite army of troops. His two concessions when reaching 65 were to give

Corky, my head man and first lieutenant. There is nothing I can add about a man who has given me 35 years of his life and total dedication.

up the Saturday afternoon and Sunday shifts, although he remains on call, and to stop riding out, which he regrets but appreciates was sensible.

Never a man to waste words, nor dispense praise without justification, he is hearing himself expressing a belief he thought beyond reality. Mentioning a chaser in the same sentence as the mighty Flyingbolt. He believes Sprinter Sacre is at least on a par and, in time, may prove superior. From the pragmatic Browne, that is a massive statement of conviction.

A note from history may be beneficial here for all readers the right side of 60. Flyingbolt, having won the Cheltenham Festival's Gloucestershire (Supreme) Hurdle in 1964, returned to take the Cotswold (Arkle) Chase in 1965. The following season he won the Champion Chase by 15 lengths. So far the story is quite similar to Sprinter Sacre's, but within 24 hours of Flyingbolt winning his Champion Chase he finished third in the Champion Hurdle and would have won under a more adventurous ride. He ended his season winning the Irish Grand National (3m2f).

Flyingbolt also features in the storyline of Bobs Worth, the first horse since to win three different prizes at successive Festivals.

'The guv'nor didn't get the credit he deserved for the Gold Cup,' says Browne. 'It was the act of a genius. Bobs Worth isn't the easiest to train. To bring him to a peak for the Hennessy after a nine-month break and then to do so again three months later for the Gold Cup was a remarkable achievement. You have to know the horse to appreciate how remarkable.

'I know outsiders will say we've got all these good horses at Seven Barrows and therefore it must be easy winning the big races, but you have to get them there for the day. It's so easy to ruin good horses by either underdoing them or overdoing them. He gets it right season after season by always doing what's best for the horse.'

Browne answers the obvious question about whether they have arguments with a smile and another question. 'Will a married couple have the occasional disagreement along the way? I think they do.'

Their association, one of the longest in racing, is built on mutual respect.

'The thing is he'll always put the horse first, no matter what,' says Browne. 'Believe me, if we arrive at the final day of the season needing another £20 of prize-money to win the championship, he wouldn't run one for the sake of it. The horse would have to be 100 per cent right for that race. He's always thinking of next season.'

But what would it mean to win the championship again? 'I'm glad you said again, because people seem to have forgotten we've had the title on two previous occasion, in the See You Then years,' he grins. 'Of course, it would be great and recognition of all the hard work everyone has put in.'

The title would be fitting, as this is the 50th anniversary of Browne's arrival in Lambourn. After a five-year apprenticeship with Kevin Kerr in County Meath, he joined the team of fledgling trainer Fred Winter. His life took a turn for the better the night he went ten-pin bowling in Swindon with a fresh-faced couple stepping out together, jockey Richard Pitman and Jenny Harvey, who was to become the first Mrs P. 'Richard kept grumbling at me because my concentration diverted to this very pretty girl bowling in the next lane. Richard said she was far too gorgeous for me and offered me 50-1 she'd turn me down for a date.' They were married 18 months later.

Corky keeps a close eye on Binocular as Jake Loader puts the 2010 Champion Hurdle winner through his paces on the gallops. He has always adored Binocular and like me felt he never got the luck or the recognition he deserved.

'Diane came racing for the first time when I took Anglo to Aintree for the National in 1966. In the horsebox on the journey there I told her if the horse won we'd get married. That was the best result of my life.'

His worst moment on a racecourse came 40 years ago next month when Killiney, whom he looked after at Winter's and adored, broke a shoulder in Ascot's Heinz Chase. He had won his eight previous races over fences, including Cheltenham's Totalisator Champion (RSA) Chase without being seriously challenged.

'I was so heartbroken I cried all the way home: who wouldn't have? Did I get over it? No. I never will. Killiney was a freak. A big machine. He was the future Arkle. The guv'nor knew he was better than Pendil. He'd been entered for the Gold Cup with Pendil and was third favourite, but the guv'nor was against running a novice in it. He said he'd probably win, but there was a danger it would be too much for him.'

After Ascot, Browne was all for quitting racing. 'The irony was he almost didn't run that day because of the fast ground. In fact, at one stage I think it was decided not to run. That night there was a knock on my front door at 8pm. It was Fred Winter with a bottle of brandy. We sat down and finished it off. I'll never forget his words: "I understand how you feel because we've lost the best we've trained, the best we've seen. We're all heartbroken. But I want you back, be it tomorrow, next week, next month, or next year. Take as long as you like, but come back."

'I woke up next morning and thought, well if it's not today it will be tomorrow, so I might as well go to work. When I arrived the lads had shut the top door of Killiney's box.'

After 13 seasons with Winter, Browne left out of financial necessity as he had two young children. 'They were laying a water pipeline in Lambourn and the pay on the job was good. Afterwards I worked for Roger Charlton for three years at his equine pool at Windsor House.'

Then, one Friday night, there was a knock at the door. It was the soon-to-train Henderson on a head-hunting assignment. The rest, as they say, is history.

Browne on...

Sprinter Sacre

When he first cantered we thought he's either a bit free or he's very good. He turned out to be both. I never reckoned I'd see a chaser as good as Flyingbolt, but this one is, if not better. As he came up the hill at Cheltenham I thought three miles wouldn't be a problem. I suppose the place to try that would be the King George. He has a huge public following. There was such a roar for him at the Festival that couldn't have been because racegoers were making money off a 1-4 shot.

Bobs Worth

He's so supremely game and will put everything into his race, but he wouldn't be the easiest to train. He can go wrong and indeed did go a bit funny between the Hennessy and the Gold Cup. He's not a horse to be rushed, you have to wait for him.

Long Run

He's a tough horse who takes his work well. His brilliant record speaks for itself. The King George twice, a Gold Cup, twice placed in a Gold Cup. They'll be more big days for him too.

Simonsig

He's very talented and we've yet to see the best of him. He did superbly well to win the Arkle because his scope was badly wrong afterwards. The way he came up the hill it was obvious that something was amiss. He's so much better than that.

Captain Conan

Big and powerful, I've always thought the world of him and my faith wasn't shaken by his defeat at the Festival. I believe two miles is his trip, but there was little point in taking on Simonsig in the Arkle.

Binocular

I've always considered him to be special, but he hasn't been the luckiest of horses. He may be tried over a fence, but sometimes the longer the top-class hurdlers remain over hurdles the more difficult it is for them to make the switch.

Captain Conan got Aintree off to a perfect start with a third Grade 1 victory of the season, which was great for the Hanburys because they love having runners there. Lee Mottershead reported:

AINTREE

APRIL 4, 2013

Beftred Manifesto Novices' Chase 2m4f

1 Captain Conan   6-5f
Barry Geraghty

2 Tap Night   8-1
AP McCoy

3 Changing Times   9-2
Sam Twiston-Davies

Distances 3¼l, 6l

For a number of reasons Wednesday morning was fraught for Nicky Henderson, but it was also the morning on which the season's leading trainer executed a change of mind that yesterday resulted in the imposing Captain Conan securing his fourth Grade 1 success. Since finishing fifth in the Jewson Novices' Chase, the Hanbury family-owned six-year-old had been earmarked for a drop back to 2m for tomorrow's Maghull Novices' Chase.

That was until a voice in Henderson's head told him to do something different, and by acting on that voice he sent out the clear-cut winner of the John Smith's Manifesto Novices' Chase.

Built like a barbarian, Captain Conan – whose three
previous Grade 1 triumphs had all come at Sandown –
looks sure to get better with age, but he is already more
than useful, as he showed by justifying 6-5 favouritism
and beating Tap Night by three and a quarter lengths
under Barry Geraghty.

'I was very indecisive and had a change of mind yesterday
morning,' said Henderson. 'Fortunately Christopher and
Bridget [Hanbury] were on a plane so we couldn't debate
it even more.

'I was always going to go down the two-mile route on
Saturday but then I looked at the two races and just thought
that this seemed a touch easier, with Overturn and Alderwood
going for the Maghull.

'It's worked out because he has jumped great and won
well. He is now finished for the season, and he has a future.
Next season will be more difficult but at least he's shown
today that he stays.'

**Friday was a great day with four winners, starting off
with My Tent Or Yours in the opening novice hurdle.
David Baxter reported:**

AINTREE

APRIL 5, 2013

Rose Appeal Supports Alder
Hey Top Novices' Hurdle
2m ½f

1 My Tent Or Yours   4-11f
AP McCoy

2 Forgotten Voice   9-2
Barry Geraghty

3 Zuider Zee   11-1
Denis O'Regan

Distances 16l, 6l

The players may change but the game remains the same for
Nicky Henderson as he saddled a one-two for the second
consecutive year in the Rose Appeal Supports Alder Hey Top
Novices' Hurdle, with My Tent Or Yours proving different
class to his three rivals, led home by Forgotten Voice.

Last year it was Darlan who came into the race as the
Supreme Novices' runner-up and defeated Captain Conan
here. Roll forward 12 months, and My Tent Or Yours,
this season's Supreme Novices' second, strolled home by
16 lengths.

Tony McCoy's mount again demonstrated a high cruising
speed, ending the race as a contest between three and two out,
and bookmakers took the opportunity to clip the six-year-old
to a general 6-1 from as big as 8-1 for next year's Champion
Hurdle.

However, the prospect of a novice chasing campaign will
be discussed by Henderson, McCoy and owner JP McManus,

My Tent Or Yours cruises home in the Top Novices' Hurdle at Aintree under AP. Forgotten Voice, who finished a distant second, would later have his day in the sunshine at Royal Ascot and Glorious Goodwood.

with jockey and trainer raising the possibility that fences could be tackled sooner rather than later.

'He'll jump a fence if we want him to, but I'd like to talk to AP and see what he thinks,' Henderson said. 'This time last year we were here with Darlan and we were dreaming about Champion Hurdles. Okay, the nice thing is we're back exactly where we were a year ago with another horse.'

McCoy was of a similar opinion, saying: 'He a good traveller and nimble jumper, a big horse. Unlike Binocular and Straw Bear he's got the size and scope to jump a fence. I did think he was a good thing at Cheltenham; today was just a case of getting around, very straightforward.'

For Forgotten Voice, winner of the Royal Hunt Cup at Ascot in 2009, the slightly slower ground, which was changed to good to soft, good in places (from good, good to soft in places) following the race, blunted his chances.

Henderson said: 'He's run a good race but just by putting that bit of water on it's slowed it up and he's a genuine fast-ground horse. If they give him half a chance we'll look at the Swinton.'

It was Sprinter Sacre who was the star of the show on the second day as he stepped up to two and a half miles for the first time. Lee Mottershead again reported:

John Smith's Melling
Chase 2m4f

1 Sprinter Sacre   1-3f
Barry Geraghty

2 Cue Card   7-1
Joe Tizzard

3 Flemenstar   7-1
Andrew Lynch

Distances 4½l, 19l

Among the heaving hordes at Aintree was a small Irishman of a certain age, here in Liverpool with his wife for their annual visit to the Grand National meeting. As a man who had known Arkle better than most, he was eminently capable of passing judgement on the horse whose remarkable talent had once again beggared belief. Paddy Woods recognised what he had seen. So did we all.

Through the most celebrated career in jump racing history, Woods was the man who rode Arkle each and every morning. He knows how an outstanding horse feels in the hands and he knows how an outstanding horse looks to the eye.

After Sprinter Sacre had humiliated not one but two exceptional rivals in Cue Card and Flemenstar, the human link to the greatest jumps horse there has ever been delivered a mighty plaudit.

'He's definitely the best I've seen since Arkle,' said Woods. 'He looks magnificent and is the complete package. He has everything.'

Among the everything that Sprinter Sacre possesses is the ability to stay two and a half miles. Prior to yesterday's John Smith's Melling Chase, we knew from two exhilarating displays at the Cheltenham Festival that he was untouchable over two miles. Now he know he is untouchable over further.

For a moment turning for home Barry Geraghty was forced to move a muscle, but a moment is all it was. From there to the line racing's most precious equine asset was sublime, first eyeballing Ryanair Chase winner Cue Card, who had made much of the running, before sauntering clear for a four-and-a-half-length success at prohibitive, but ultimately generous, odds of 1-3. A long 19 lengths back in third was Ireland's bright hope Flemenstar, humbled but with reputation intact.

'It's a joy now it's over, but during the race my eyes were shut,' said trainer Nicky Henderson, whose 2012 Melling winner Finian's Rainbow ran his best race of the season in fourth.

'We had to make up a bit of ground on a very good horse in Cue Card, but it didn't seem too difficult. This fellow loves what he's doing and I'm conscious he's something to be enjoyed. I'm the custodian, and lucky to be the custodian of a spectacular horse. I must try to bring him back to the racecourse as often as I can.'

Sprinter Sacre and Barry jump the final fence with a clear lead in the John Smith's Melling Chase on his first start over two and a half miles. To him it was another day at the office, but to us it was another bridge crossed.

There is a possibility the next racecourse trip could come as soon as the opening day of the Punchestown Festival. 'I've promised I'll take him to Ireland one day,' said Henderson, who seemed less keen on a further step up in trip for the William Hill King George VI Chase, for which the sponsors make him 6-4 favourite.

'We wouldn't think about a King George at this particular moment,' he said, adding: 'I think today's trip is as far as he needs to go.'

At this trip he is magnificent, as Geraghty knows best. 'He did what we thought he'd do,' he said. 'The distance was no concern to me. We've come to expect great performances from him and we got a great performance. It's just brilliant. He's a great horse and I love riding him.'

For Geraghty, the whole Sprinter Sacre experience is pure pleasure. Not so for Henderson. Nor for owner Caroline Mould.

'You always want a horse like this, but when you have one it's a very different ball game,' she said. 'I had the window

Sprinter Sacre is the centre of attention in Aintree's winner's enclosure. I know he is quite a show-off, but I don't think even Sprinter would have written that on his rug! It was another stunning performance and reception afterwards.

down in the car coming to Aintree because I thought I was going to be sick. You have reservations every time he runs, as it's obvious he's become public property. That brings a huge pressure.'

Asked if she feared her horse might one day be beaten, Mould nodded. 'I do, but I'm fairly fatalistic,' she said. Those connected with the vanquished must view the possibility of the sacred one ever being defeated as extremely doubtful.

'I'm as proud as hell of Cue Card,' said rider Joe Tizzard, while trainer-father Colin, who will now send his stable star on holiday, observed: 'Sprinter Sacre is the best I've seen and to me would stay any trip. I don't think I'd be in a hurry to take him on again. Once a year is enough!'

As it almost certainly will be for the Punchestown-bound Flemenstar. 'The plain and simple truth is that he just was not good enough,' said trainer Peter Casey's son Francis. 'There are no excuses. He'll win plenty of Grade 1s in Ireland and nine times out of ten he'd have won that race.'

Then, just as compatriot Paddy Woods had done, Casey harked back to another age. 'After 50 years,' he said, 'you're finally getting your own back on us for Arkle kicking the s*** out of you.'

And no matter where you hail from, watching him kick is a wonderful delight.

I had said all year that Triolo D'Alene was a Topham horse and he didn't disappoint. It was great for Sandy and Caroline Orr, who own him, because it was the first time they had had a runner in a feature race. The victory meant a lot to them. Jon Lees reported:

AINTREE

APRIL 5, 2013

John Smith's Topham Chase Handicap 2m 5½f

1 Triolo D'Alene   14-1
Barry Geraghty

2 Walkon   16-1
Wayne Hutchinson

3 Last Time D'Albain   16-1
Bryan Cooper

4 Dunowen Point   33-1
Jason Maguire

Distances ¾l, 5l, 3l

It might have looked like the best laid plan but behind Triolo D'Alene's sure-footed performance in the John Smith's Topham Chase lay several days of soul searching.

The weekend before Triolo D'Alene was to line up for the race trainer Nicky Henderson had prepared his whole season around, he stood on a shoe, this putting the whole trip in jeopardy.

But Seven Barrows staff pulled out all the stops to get the horse right for Aintree and their efforts were rewarded when the six-year-old held the rallying Walkon by three-quarters of a length to take the £120,000 prize with Last Time D'Albain third and long-time leader Dunowen Point fourth.

While he came home first the stable's other two challengers Giorgio Quercus and State Benefit were less fortunate. Both were taken out of the race when Little Josh came down at the 15th fence, the former Paddy Power Gold Cup winner fracturing a shoulder which led to him being put down.

Henderson said: 'This has been a humungous effort by everyone at home. He has not been easy all season, he's had respiratory problems, but the last week has been a particular nightmare. I always thought this horse was made to jump these fences. Everything was going great but then literally during the night last weekend he took his shoe off and stepped on it.

'I have to pay absolute credit to everyone at home. He has been stood in poultices, buckets of ice, saltwater, foot spas. He never missed any work because of it. I was having to give the Orrs regular bulletins but in the end we got here.'

As a dress rehearsal for a return to Aintree next year Triolo D'Alene did enough to impress jockey Barry Geraghty. 'At a couple of them I asked him and he put down, he was very good. He's a young horse and could be a Grand National horse next year.'

A fourth winner of the day was landed with Minella Forfitness for Michael Buckley in the Listed hurdle. Peter Scargill reported:

AINTREE

APRIL 5, 2013

John Smith's Daily Mirror Punters Club Handicap Hurdle 2m4f

1 Minella Forfitness   10-1
David Bass

2 Clerk's Choice   33-1
Sam Twiston-Davies

3 Meister Eckhart   15-2f
Aidan Coleman

4 Manyriverstocross   10-1
Wayne Hutchinson

Distances ½l, 2½l, 3½l

In the end, winning is the most important thing, and Michael Buckley was delighted the winner was his as Minella Forfitness grabbed the Listed handicap hurdle.

The owner lost Oscar Nominee earlier this season and things have not quite gone to plan for his star Finian's Rainbow, but those setbacks were forgotten yesterday as Minella Forfitness, a 10-1 shot, gained a smooth victory.

'We all try to be happy, smiley losers, but we all want to win really,' Buckley said. 'It's boring when they don't win for a while.

'You keep trying to say "Well done" and shake hands, but you want to have the winner yourself. I have to say I'm a good loser, but I'm a really good winner too!' The win was the fourth of the afternoon for Nicky Henderson, who believes the six-year-old has a big future now he has learned to settle.

'Michael has been one of my biggest supporters and he's had a torrid season,' Henderson said. 'I'm thrilled to find him one to win at one of the big meetings.'

He added: 'The horse has tended to do too much in his races, but he's improving and becoming more professional. He'll keep getting better.'

Reviewing the day, Alastair Down believed there was no high that could not be scaled by our chasing phenomenon:

A very early Pink Floyd track entitled Set The Controls For The Heart Of The Sun came to mind watching Sprinter Sacre yesterday as something about his latent power leads you to believe he can take us anywhere and that no height or orbit is beyond his reach.

Triolo D'Alene and Barry (left) jump the last fence in the Topham Chase with Dunowen Point (Jason Maguire) who finished fourth. Triolo gave Barry a wonderful ride – and vice-versa – for our great friends Sandy and Caroline Orr. They've had horses with us for many years.

This was the best field he has faced this season, his rivals jumped well and those who could have a dart at him did so. But it was never any real form of a contest. In fact, throughout the race you felt they weren't going fast enough for Sprinter Sacre and Barry Geraghty said: 'I could have done with them going quicker – I had to take him back a few times and couldn't really use his jumping.'

Crucially for the future course charted for this phenomenon, Geraghty added: 'He is very manageable and he is never one to do anything stupid and tear off with you.'

This, of course, opens up options, although after the race Nicky Henderson seemed to rule out going further than this two and a half miles which would remove the possibility of a King George bid.

But this horse's amenability might mean that if he goes on knocking seven bells out of everything over two and two a half miles then eventually the Seven Barrows brains trust might think of having a pop at Kempton on Boxing Day. The initial reaction to this victory was that longer trips are firmly within Sprinter Sacre's scope and Colin Tizzard simply said of the winner: 'He'd win over any trip, wouldn't he?'

Tizzard admitted he won't be in a blinding rush to take Sprinter Sacre on again with Cue Card, but he can be hugely proud of his horse, who in his two clashes with Henderson's charge has finished seven lengths behind him in last year's Arkle and four and half lengths adrift here. That is two hugely creditable runs, although yesterday's winning margin could have been extended massively at a click of Geraghty's fingers.

Henderson had a four-timer yesterday, starting with My Tent Or Yours in a £60,000 egg-and-spoon race that opened the card and then rattling in the Sprinter, Triolo D'Alene and Minella Forfitness. Graham Cunningham, newly installed as the *Racing Post*'s Friday columnist, highlighted to me the extent of Henderson's dominance at the Cheltenham Festival and Aintree Grand National meeting over the last two years.

At the Festival Henderson had seven winners in 2012 and four last month. Twelve months ago he saddled six winners here at Aintree and has had five over the first two days this week.

That means that out of a total of 89 races he has won 22 of them – a 25 per cent strike-rate at the two most fiercely contested meetings of the year in the teeth of the very finest Ireland has to offer, let alone the massed bands of the best of British. It is an extraordinary record at the highest level possible.

And happy to relate Henderson seems keen Sprinter Sacre does his stuff in public with a degree of frequency that has gone out of fashion with top-class horses in recent years. He even suggested Sprinter Sacre might go to Punchestown, although that plan seemed to have stalled a bit by the end of the afternoon.

But be in no doubt he will be sent over to Ireland at some stage because Henderson believes Sprinter Sacre is a joy to be shared and, given he hardly seems to take anything out of himself in his races, he could probably run once a week and twice on Sundays. Great horses are evangelists for this sport and the more we see them the better.

At last, something for Michael Buckley to smile about, when Minella Forfitness and Barry (left) clear the final flight in the lead in the Listed hurdle to complete a four-timer for Seven Barrows on the Friday at Aintree.

It really sank in about the championship on the Friday of Aintree, because thank God even the Grand National wouldn't have won it for Paul Nicholls by then. It became a realistic eventuality and of course I wanted to win it, although for much of the season I'd been saying that I was going to let it look after itself because I didn't want it being the main focus.

We sometimes take the horses for an away day, but we didn't go very far on this day as we went to the Jockey Club Estates gallops at Mandown in Lambourn, which is adjacent to our schooling grounds. It's always fun when owners come to watch their horses and here are Simon Munir (left), Brian Stewart-Brown and Michael Buckley on what looks like a pretty unpleasant morning.

David Minton and I have worked together virtually from day one, and he has been an enormous friend and ally throughout the whole journey. His passion for National Hunt racing and breeding is unparalleled.

At that stage of the season everyone becomes very good at maths, and until that Aintree Friday I was always looking for a way it might slip away. Winning the title again gives me great satisfaction and it gives the yard a big boost – it was a race for the title and we won that race. It was a big team effort that was well rewarded.

Minty worked out that as far as regaining a championship after 26 years was concerned, the only one he could find in the same ballpark as ours was George Foreman, who regained the world heavyweight crown after 21 years – that was second-best as far as length of time went, but I think George probably had a harder task than I did!

The most important thing of the whole week, though, was that the Grand National went off without a hitch. I think everyone did a very good job. Dad was one of the people who helped to save it and it is our job to keep it going and protect it. We haven't managed to win it yet and our luck wasn't in this year as Roberto Goldback unseated Barry, but we'll be back again in 2014.

After Aintree two of my key allies, David Minton and Michael Buckley, reflected on the championship success with Graham Green:

Leading bloodstock agent David Minton yesterday predicted the start of a new era at the head of the jumping ranks after Nicky Henderson finally ended Paul Nicholls' seven-year stranglehold on the trainers' championship.

Twelve months ago, Neptune Collonges' Aintree triumph secured the title for Nicholls after an epic battle with his rival, but with both missing out on Saturday's last major prize of the campaign, the master of Seven Barrows enjoys the luxury of entering the final three weeks of the season holding an unassailable advantage of more than £500,000.

Despite having been at the top of his profession for more than a quarter of a century, Henderson has previously only won the crown twice, the last time in the 1986–87 season.

Minton, whose many Henderson-trained purchases include Bobs Worth and Sprinter Sacre, said: 'I'm delighted for Nicky and all his team, and I feel honoured to have been involved with him since he started training in 1978. Obviously, with the star horses he has this year, and hopefully going on for a few seasons, he could go on and win several more championships after this.

'Nicky isn't a person who shows the championship means much to him, but it certainly did last year. He thought he was home and hosed before Paul won the National, and that just made him more determined to win it this year.'

Michael Buckley, who has had horses with Henderson since 1983, including Finian's Rainbow, said: 'It is a terrific achievement to win the title back after such a long time, and from my point of view as a really good friend, I'm really happy and proud for him.

'He and his family have done so much for the sport. I'm also delighted for Corky Browne who has been with Nicky since the day he started, and they are really joined at the hip if not other places as well.'

Although the championship was sealed, the season wasn't finished as Sprinter travelled to Ireland. I can say now that the day he ran at Punchestown, and the three days afterwards, provided one of the most incredible experiences of my whole life. It was the high spot of the whole year and I'll never, ever forget it.

I said at Cheltenham that he would probably go to Punchestown, and their racing manager Richie Galway, who is married to Emma Harrington, daughter of Johnny and Jessie Harrington, was doing everything to get us there; there were carrots flying everywhere. I expect he was horrified when a week later I came out and said I'd changed my mind and we'd run him at Aintree first. I did want to try him over two and a half miles, because if he did get the trip then of course we'd have so many more options.

That was a complete afterthought, because I'd always said that I wanted to take him to Ireland as we all love Punchestown anyway, and the Irish are so passionate about their horses and their racing and they've always been very good to us. I felt it was right that Sprinter went over there at some stage of his life. Then a week before Punchestown his trach wash came up slightly messy, and I didn't make a firm decision until the Friday before the race.

Justin O'Hanlon reported as Sprinter Sacre made it five out of five for the season:

PUNCHESTOWN
APRIL 23, 2013

Boylesports.com
Champion Chase 2m

1 Sprinter Sacre   1-9f
Barry Geraghty

2 Sizing Europe   6-1
Andrew Lynch

3 Days Hotel   20-1
Phillip Enright

Distances 5½l, 33l

A perfect ten out of ten over fences, a third Grade 1 chase success in six weeks and the first horse since Istabraq to win at the Cheltenham, Aintree and Punchestown festivals.

The positive effect of having a superstar like Sprinter Sacre on the jump racing scene is incalculable, but it was given some visual context by the sight of a record first-day crowd of 18,607 cheering him back in after his victory in the Boylesports.com Champion Chase in scenes the likes of which have not been witnessed at the Punchestown Festival since Dawn Run beat Buck House in The Match in 1986.

Winning rider Barry Geraghty provided his personal comparison when saying he had not experienced anything like it since watching Desert Orchid win the Irish Grand National at Fairyhouse when the jockey was just ten years of age.

But it wasn't plain sailing. A stop-start gallop was set by former champion Sizing Europe and the old warrior managed to take Sprinter Sacre to the last and forced him to be at least shaken up for a few strides before proper order was restored. The 19 lengths from Cheltenham were narrowed to a mere five and a half lengths this time, but it was obvious the 11-year-old Sizing Europe had run his heart out while the new young champion had suffered no more than a minor inconvenience.

'It was tougher today, but he was at his best at Cheltenham, he wasn't quite as sharp at Aintree and he's probably not as sharp today,' said trainer Nicky Henderson. 'You have to have him peaked for Cheltenham, but then to come back and then come back again – it takes a very good horse to do it.

'You might think he's getting easy races, but when you keep bringing him into these theatres it has to take a lot out of them. To do the three is very, very hard.'

Although any worries about the ground were ultimately dispelled, the conditions did not really play to Sprinter Sacre's strengths.

Henderson said: 'If you get him on really good two-mile ground and get him jumping he's absolutely spectacular. He couldn't quite do that out of this ground. When he was Tingle

Creeking and Victor Chandlering he just winged his way around. He didn't do anything wrong. He was clinical and clean. Just a very good horse.'

On the reception the horse received on his first visit to Ireland, Henderson added: 'It was special. We love coming here, we've been doing it for years. This is a nation of horse lovers and if you have a stunning horse like this you feel you owe it to everybody to come. There's no point leaving him at home.'

As for next season's campaign, Henderson said: 'It will be the same plan next year,' although Geraghty wasn't dismissive of the prospect of Sprinter Sacre staying three miles. Paddy Power quoted him as a 7-2 chance for next year's Gold Cup while offering 1-4 for him to retain his Champion Chase crown.

Geraghty said: 'He's a brilliant two-miler, he's won over two and a half miles, the world is his oyster and he has all the options. We'll just enjoy today and worry about the King George nearer Christmas!'

Sponsors William Hill make him a 6-4 favourite for the King George.

The role Sizing Europe played in this contest shouldn't be forgotten and it was as good a performance as he has put in for some time.

'The plan was to throw the kitchen sink at Sprinter Sacre and that's exactly what we did,' said trainer Henry de Bromhead. 'It's really nice to see us getting Sprinter Sacre off the bridle. He's a really special horse.'

Lee Mottershead witnessed a horse for the ages at Punchestown:

The horse is here but the man is not. To have the horse is a joy and a privilege. He dominates the day, his name lauded over countless pints of black stuff, but although the horse, Sprinter Sacre, is present, the man, JT McNamara is absent. Quite rightly, at the start of this tremendous Festival, we are reminded of both.

Shortly after 1pm, Nicky Henderson is escorted into the track's overflow press room. It is media briefing time, just as 6pm on Monday night was media briefing time. The trainer of Sprinter Sacre makes himself available for one interview after another, the same questions asked, the same answers given.

What's that coming over the hill? It's Sprinter Sacre and Barry.

For Punchestown, all Christmases have come at once. They wanted him, they have got him and they want us to know it. Henderson, who adores this meeting and this country, is very happy to assist, but there are still four and a half hours until race time and he rather wishes there were not.

'Let's just get it on, over and done with,' he says. 'Punchestown has this great idea of running the race at 5.30pm but it just drags out the agony. I'm hoping we've brought something that Ireland will enjoy watching. I'm lucky. I have the privilege of watching him every day.'

Racegoers who watch racing only in Ireland have never seen in the flesh what Henderson sees so often. Enthusiasts like Tom Keenan, an 83-year-old from Donadea, County Kildare, will get to see him, just as he once got to see Arkle. For Keenan, who has seen much in between, this is a similarly momentous experience.

'I can't wait,' he says, settled comfortably on a bench. 'I've been coming to Punchestown for 64, maybe 65, years and I've never seen one better than Sprinter Sacre, not over his distance anyway.

'Arkle was the best there's been over three miles and watching him here in those days was unreal. I've not come here as excited about a horse since then. I think he'll win by about ten lengths – and he'll do it on the bridle.'

With Barry and Sprinter Sacre after the race. We even managed to persuade Corky (right) to come with us to show his horse to his countrymen.

Tom and a friend resume their conversation. All around the racecourse similar conversations are being had. In this small nugget of the racing world the talk is not of anabolic steroids, scandal and shame, but of a very special horse and what he might do a little later in the day. Expectant racegoers exchange thoughts about Sprinter Sacre and then, when they reach a trade stand by the corner of the paddock, they begin talking of something else. The stand promotes The Jockeys Emergency Fund and by it are two huge greetings cards, one addressed to John Thomas McNamara, the other to Jonjo Bright. Neither man is here but neither man is being forgotten.

Encouragingly, Bright has regained movement in his arms since the point-to-point accident that changed his life. McNamara, twice the age of the teenager at 38, has been left paralysed by his Cheltenham Festival fall. He was the one with the fame and he is the one whose absence hits home when Zest For Life, once ridden to a point-to-point success by the Punchestown legend, wins the opening banks race for McNamara's long-time friend and supporter Enda Bolger.

'That was amazing. It's the best day of my life,' says 18-year-old rider Tim Donworth, for whom this is a first win.

More accustomed to success, not least at Punchestown, is Bolger. This time, however, it is a little different. 'Not having John Thomas makes this is the strangest Punchestown I've known,' he says.

'He is like a younger brother to me. I think about him every hour. The good thing is he's in great spirits and he has a fantastic wife and fantastic friends. This is a man who is going to battle.'

For a few anxious moments Sprinter Sacre also comes close to a battle.

From the start, the Champion Chase concerns only two horses. As one former champion enters the home straight, closely followed by an exceptional current champion, Barry Geraghty begins to look a little more energetic than we had expected. Brilliance has been blunted by the exertions of Cheltenham and Aintree but the sacred one still pulls through, not at his peak but still five and a half lengths better than the horse who before him was best. For Henderson, the agony is over.

They wait for his return, necks craned, cameras pointed. Only those of a certain vintage, only those with memories like Keenan, can remember seeing a finer creature on this Kildare soil. Then, smiles all around, glasses are charged, to absent friends and a wonderful horse, unforgettable memories on the day Sprinter came to Ireland.

It was quite extraordinary. It was a like a party that went on for three days. People have told me that they'd never seen scenes on an Irish racecourse like that. Sprinter Sacre always wears earplugs, and it's just as well he does because they were applauding him even as he walked into the parade ring. He's a great showoff, he can cope with it. For three days I found out what football players and film stars go through. Everyone on the racecourse seemed to come up to me to say thank you for bringing him.

Punchestown rounded off an amazing year. At the beginning of the season everyone thought we would or could win the title, but it still had to happen.

Paul Nicholls and I have always been good mates and it has been a friendly rivalry for the last two years. It has only taken 26 years to get the title back!

We're very lucky to have such a great bunch of horses and owners. They couldn't belong to better people and we have a team at home who are everything. It's all worked and gelled. The horses performed to their best when they had to and it's come off.

It's a long time ago since this last happened. A comeback is a bit weird but we've been knocking on the door and it's nice to finish back on top. When you get good horses it's amazing how they bring each other on. As far as the trainers' championship is concerned the only thing you ask is for horses to be in good form and good health. You have to win races like the Hennessy and King George – I have had a lot of luck.

When it happened it was great and on the last day when the prizes were handed out at Sandown Park it was wonderful because everyone was present. Paul Nicholls was there and, although we are all competitive, we are all mates. The next day we went back to zero and off we go again.

However, it didn't end there as we had some success on the Flat. As I said right at the start, we select a little team

The end of the season and a very proud moment for me and my three daughters, Camilla (left), Sarah and Tessa.

of horses who I think we can have some fun with. For Royal Ascot 2013 we had Lieutenant Miller, who finished third in the Ascot Stakes, and Forgotten Voice, who won the Wolferton Handicap.

I had wanted to run Forgotten Voice in the Swinton Hurdle at Haydock in May but the ground was too soft and we pulled him out. I persuaded owner Paul Roy to run on the Flat and Johnny Murtagh, who had ridden the horse to win the Hunt Cup at the royal meeting in 2009, gave a him a great ride in the Wolferton.

Forgotten Voice then won what I think was our first Group race on the Flat in the Glorious Stakes at Goodwood – it's always good to nick a few good races off the Flat boys! That ended a wonderful year but, as I write this in September 2013, the horses have come back after their holidays, and it's time to start all over again …

Overleaf: In the winner's enclosure after Forgotten Voice won the Wolferton Stakes at Royal Ascot.

WINNERS, 2012–13

The list below records all Nicky Henderson's winners in Great Britain and Ireland during the 2012–13 jumps season, with Grade 1 winners highlighted.

DATE	HORSE	OWNER	JOCKEY	RACECOURSE
May				
11th	City Press	Trevor Hemmings	Barry Geraghty	Market Rasen
11th	Close Touch	HM The Queen	Barry Geraghty	Market Rasen
12th	Polly Peachum	Lady Tennant	David Bass	Warwick
15th	Cape Express	Alan Spence	Andrew Tinkler	Southwell
16th	Pippa Greene	RAH Evans	Andrew Tinkler	Fontwell
16th	Lieutenant Miller	Henry Ponsonby	Andrew Tinkler	Fontwell
19th	Master Of The Game	Richard Kelvin Hughes	Andrew Tinkler	Bangor
20th	Carabinier	The Girls Syndicate	Jeremiah McGrath	Market Rasen
21st	Zama Zama	Michael Buckley	AP McCoy	Newton Abbot
21st	Billy Twyford	Simon Munir	Jeremiah McGrath	Newton Abbot
31st	Seaham Hall	Seasons Holidays	Andrew Tinkler	Ffos Las
June				
5th	Your Tepee Or Mine	The Happy Campers	Andrew Tinkler	Ffos Las
6th	Rackham Lerouge	Judy Wilson	AP McCoy	Fontwell
6th	Heronry	The Ten From Seven	AP McCoy	Fontwell
12th	Spartan Angel	Sir Eric Parker & Mary Anne Parker	David Bass	Southwell
14th	One Conemara	Triermore Stud	Andrew Tinkler	Uttoxeter
24th	Cape Express	Alan Spence	David Bass	Hereford
July				
15th	Springinherstep	Turf Club	David Bass	Southwell
24th	Forgotten Voice	Susan Roy	AP McCoy	Bangor
25th	Cape Express	Alan Spence	Andrew Tinkler	Worcester

DATE	HORSE	OWNER	JOCKEY	RACECOURSE
August				
3rd	First In The Queue	Liam Breslin	AP McCoy	Bangor
16th	Laudatory	Eric Newnham & Julia Newnham	Edmond Linehan	Stratford
18th	Forgotten Voice	Susan Roy	AP McCoy	Market Rasen
October				
19th	Makari	Matt & Lauren Morgan	Andrew Tinkler	Fakenham
20th	Nadiya De La Vega	JP McManus	AP McCoy	Cheltenham
26th	Close Touch	HM The Queen	Barry Geraghty	Fakenham
27th	Cape Express	Alan Spence	Barry Geraghty	Aintree
29th	Karazhan	Pump & Plant Services Ltd	David Bass	Bangor
30th	Molotof	Simon Munir	AP McCoy	Taunton
31st	Ma Filleule	Simon Munir	David Bass	Haydock
November				
1st	Vasco Du Ronceray	Simon Munir & Isaac Souede	AP McCoy	Hereford
1st	Polly Peachum	Lady Tennant	Andrew Tinkler	Stratford
1st	Cevaro	Seven Barrows Limited	Mr Jack Sherwood	Hereford
3rd	Hadrian's Approach	Richard Kelvin Hughes	Barry Geraghty	Ascot
3rd	My Tent Or Yours	JP McManus	AP McCoy	Ascot
3rd	Une Artiste	Simon Munir	Jeremiah McGrath	Wetherby
3rd	Roberto Goldback	Simon Munir	Barry Geraghty	Ascot
5th	Golden Hoof	Andrew Chandler & Lee Westwood	Andrew Tinkler	Kempton
15th	Karazhan	Pump & Plant Services Ltd	David Bass	Ludlow
18th	Captain Conan	Triermore Stud	Barry Geraghty	Cheltenham
19th	Broadbackbob	Anthony Speelman	Barry Geraghty	Plumpton
23rd	Minella Class	Deal, George, Kelvin Hughes, Nicholson	Barry Geraghty	Ascot
23rd	Close Touch	HM The Queen	Barry Geraghty	Ascot
23rd	Petit Robin	SW Group Logistics Limited	Barry Geraghty	Ascot
24th	Oscar Whisky	Walters Plant Hire Ltd	Barry Geraghty	Ascot
29th	Lyvius	Trevor Hemmings	Barry Geraghty	Newbury

DATE	HORSE	OWNER	JOCKEY	RACECOURSE
December				
1st	Bobs Worth	The Not Afraid Partnership	Barry Geraghty	Newbury
2nd	Free Thinking	Robert Waley-Cohen	Mr Sam Waley-Cohen	Kempton
7th	State Benefit	Michael Buckley	Mr Nico de Boinville	Sandown
8th	Golden Hoof	Andrew Chandler & Lee Westwood	Barry Geraghty	Sandown
8th	Captain Conan	Triermore Stud	Barry Geraghty	Sandown
8th	Petit Robin	SW Group Logistics Limited	Mr Nico de Boinville	Sandown
8th	Bear's Affair	George and Anne Barlow	Jeremiah McGrath	Aintree
8th	Sprinter Sacre	Caroline Mould	Barry Geraghty	Sandown
10th	Ericht	Bridget Hanbury	Gary Derwin	Fakenham
15th	Oscar Whisky	Walters Plant Hire Ltd	Barry Geraghty	Cheltenham
21st	Simonsig	Ronnie Bartlett	Barry Geraghty	Ascot
21st	Captain Cutter	Sue Magnier	Barry Geraghty	Ascot
26th	Whisper	Walters Plant Hire Ltd	Andrew Tinkler	Ffos Las
26th	River Maigue	Michael Buckley	Barry Geraghty	Kempton
26th	Rajdhani Express	Robert Waley-Cohen	Mr Sam Waley-Cohen	Kempton
26th	Darlan	JP McManus	AP McCoy	Kempton
26th	Long Run	Robert Waley-Cohen	Mr Sam Waley-Cohen	Kempton
27th	Simonsig	Ronnie Bartlett	Barry Geraghty	Kempton
29th	Chatterbox	The Not Afraid Partnership 2	Barry Geraghty	Newbury
January				
5th	Une Artiste	Simon Munir	Barry Geraghty	Sandown
9th	Oscar Hoof	The Hoof Partnership	Andrew Tinkler	Ludlow
11th	My Tent Or Yours	JP McManus	AP McCoy	Huntingdon
11th	Malt Master	JP McManus	AP McCoy	Huntingdon
11th	Glorious Twelfth	Richard Kelvin Hughes	AP McCoy	Huntingdon
12th	Tetlami	Susan Roy	Barry Geraghty	Kempton
12th	Oscara Dara	BG Racing Partnership	Barry Geraghty	Kempton
25th	Ericht	Bridget Hanbury	Barry Geraghty	Kempton
26th	Rolling Star	Michael Buckley & The Vestey Family	Barry Geraghty	Cheltenham
26th	Sprinter Sacre	Caroline Mould	Barry Geraghty	Cheltenham
27th	Karazhan	Pump & Plant Services Ltd	David Bass	Wolverhampton

DATE	HORSE	OWNER	JOCKEY	RACECOURSE

February

DATE	HORSE	OWNER	JOCKEY	RACECOURSE
2nd	Captain Conan	Triermore Stud	Barry Geraghty	Sandown
4th	Utopie Des Bordes	Simon Munir & Isaac Souede	Barry Geraghty	Doncaster
4th	Minella Forfitness	Michael Buckley	Barry Geraghty	Doncaster
6th	One Conemara	Triermore Stud	Andrew Tinkler	Ludlow
8th	Golden Hoof	The Hoof Partnership	Andrew Tinkler	Bangor
8th	Ericht	Bridget Hanbury	Barry Geraghty	Kempton
8th	Prince Of Pirates	JP McManus	AP McCoy	Kempton
8th	Tradewinds	Michael Buckley	Barry Geraghty	Kempton
9th	Chatterbox	The Not Afraid Partnership 2	Barry Geraghty	Newbury
9th	Ma Filleule	Simon Munir	AP McCoy	Warwick
9th	Molotof	Simon Munir	David Bass	Warwick
9th	My Tent Or Yours	JP McManus	AP McCoy	Newbury
15th	Utopie Des Bordes	Simon Munir & Isaac Souede	Barry Geraghty	Sandown
15th	Heronry	The Ten From Seven	Barry Geraghty	Sandown
15th	Free Thinking	Robert Waley-Cohen	Mr Sam Waley-Cohen	Fakenham
17th	Whisper	Walters Plant Hire Ltd	Andrew Tinkler	Ffos Las
20th	Otto The Great	John Cotton	Barry Geraghty	Doncaster
20th	Minella Forfitness	Michael Buckley	Barry Geraghty	Doncaster
21st	Tetlami	Susan Roy	Barry Geraghty	Huntingdon
21st	Miss Ballantyne	Richard Kelvin Hughes	Barry Geraghty	Huntingdon
23rd	Forgotten Voice	Susan Roy	Barry Geraghty	Kempton
28th	Who's Cross	Declan Donohoe	Andrew Tinkler	Ludlow

March

DATE	HORSE	OWNER	JOCKEY	RACECOURSE
1st	Fabrika	Richard Kelvin Hughes	Barry Geraghty	Newbury
3rd	Shernando	Sandy Orr	AP McCoy	Huntingdon
6th	Heronry	The Ten From Seven	AP McCoy	Fontwell
8th	Top Of The Range	Walters Plant Hire Ltd	Barry Geraghty	Sandown
9th	Close Touch	HM The Queen	Barry Geraghty	Sandown
11th	Little Dutch Girl	Judy Maitland-Jones	David Bass	Taunton
12th	Simonsig	Ronnie Bartlett	Barry Geraghty	Cheltenham
12th	Rajdhani Express	Robert Waley-Cohen	Mr Sam Waley-Cohen	Cheltenham

DATE	HORSE	OWNERS	JOCKEY	RACECOURSE
13th	Sprinter Sacre	Caroline Mould	Barry Geraghty	Cheltenham
15th	Bobs Worth	The Not Afraid Partnership	Barry Geraghty	Cheltenham
16th	Open Hearted	HM The Queen	Barry Geraghty	Kempton
16th	West Wizard	Walters Plant Hire Ltd	Barry Geraghty	Kempton

April

DATE	HORSE	OWNERS	JOCKEY	RACECOURSE
1st	Springinherstep	Turf Club 2012	David Bass	Huntingdon
1st	Private Equity	Million In Mind Partnership	Andrew Tinkler	Huntingdon
1st	Mayfair Music	Mrs E (Bunny) Roberts	Jeremiah McGrath	Fakenham
2nd	Nadiya De La Vega	JP McManus	AP McCoy	Fairyhouse
4th	Captain Conan	Triermore Stud	Barry Geraghty	Aintree
5th	My Tent Or Yours	JP McManus	AP McCoy	Aintree
5th	Sprinter Sacre	Caroline Mould	Barry Geraghty	Aintree
5th	Triolo D'Alene	Sandy Orr	Barry Geraghty	Aintree
5th	Minella Forfitness	Michael Buckley	David Bass	Aintree
16th	Polly Peachum	Lady Tennant	David Bass	Kempton
17th	Whisper	Walters Plant Hire Ltd	Barry Geraghty	Cheltenham
19th	Definite Ruby	Trevor & Linda Marlow	David Bass	Fontwell
20th	Rajdhani Express	Robert Waley-Cohen	Mr Sam Waley-Cohen	Ayr
23rd	Act Four	Triermore Stud	Andrew Tinkler	Towcester
23rd	Sprinter Sacre	Caroline Mould	Barry Geraghty	Punchestown
24th	Utopie Des Bordes	Simon Munir & Isaac Souede	David Bass	Perth
27th	Oscar Hoof	The Hoof Partnership	Jeremiah McGrath	Market Rasen

SEASONAL TOTALS, 1978–79 TO 2012–13

Jump races in Great Britain only. From 1978–79 to 1986–87 prize-money is win only.
From 1987–88 onwards prize-money is win and place.

YEAR	WINNERS	RUNNERS	PRIZE-MONEY	POSITION
1978–79	23	132	£21,253	31st
1979–80	37	206	£60,068	12th
1980–81	33	222	£39,267	25th
1981–82	29	254	£48,309	19th
1982–83	40	243	£71,264	11th
1983–84	43	265	£103,290	9th
1984–85	40	222	£148,479	5th
1985–86	46	240	£168,234	1st
1986–87	67	298	£222,924	1st
1987–88	40	242	£128,578	17th
1988–89	43	244	£229,136	8th
1989–90	41	247	£275,124	11th
1990–91	49	264	£372,098	7th
1991–92	52	251	£445,574	4th
1992–93	53	289	£331,140	8th
1993–94	48	270	£307,055	7th
1994–95	45	211	£341,801	10th
1995–96	47	278	£402,247	8th
1996–97	58	303	£350,660	8th
1997–98	54	277	£349,459	9th
1998–99	73	315	£584,008	6th
1999–2000	67	315	£864,094	4th
2000–01	81	346	£843,905	3rd
2001–02	93	417	£861,651	5th
2002–03	69	394	£1,072,158	5th

YEAR	WINNERS	RUNNERS	PRIZE-MONEY	POSITION
2003–04	79	370	£1,197,815	5th
2004–05	53	362	£731,207	9th
2005–06	85	390	£1,058,137	5th
2006–07	74	320	£990,763	6th
2007–08	83	277	£1,048,181	6th
2008–09	115	499	£2,122,857	2nd
2009–10	136	512	£2,055,480	2nd
2010–11	153	612	£2,210,465	2nd
2011–12	167	627	£2,741,455	2nd
2012–13	125	509	£2,924,917	1st

INDEX